SHATTERED LIVES

Anthony 'DOC' Hamilton

SHATTERED LIVES

Copyright 2003
Anthony Hamilton

All rights reserved. This material is protected under the copyright laws of the United States of America. This book may not be copied or reprinted for commercial gain or profit. The use of quotations or page copying for personal use is permitted and encouraged. Permission will be granted upon request from the author or publisher.

DEDICATION

This book is dedicated to
the driving force in my
life, my mother.

ACKNOWLEDGMENTS

Anthony Paul, you have been a major factor in my quest for growth. I thank you deeply for your part in cultivating the man I've become, and at the same time I ask for your forgiveness for having you when I myself was just a child. I've asked God to place inside of me a father you can be proud of and I hope that he has.

Anthony Darnell, I miss what we could have had and crave what we still can. I shall continue knocking on the door of reconciliation until you answer.

Emmanuel, words cannot describe the journeys we have endured, but I wouldn't have had it any other way. When you are in your right state of mind, the mere core of your reasoning exemplifies greatness. Never stop playing your music and never stop reaching into your bag of funk. Know that if no one else understands your funk, I do.

Toddrick, never disown the rhythm that has dazzled so many. Never lose the creativity that for years has allowed you to become the individual you are today. Remain obedient towards those true things in life, and the riches of this world shall be bestowed upon you.

Elyscia, watching you grow has been amazingly gratifying. You now possess the moral tools of emotional empowerment. Your uncanny ability to decipher the difference between what is uttered and what is fact sets my mind at ease.

My sister, Alice, thank you for caressing my heart with your smiles as I traveled through reluctant miles. I have always been moved by your spirit and by your readiness to give. But more than anything, I've always admired the way you live.

My sister, Doretha, always remember that peace costs so little, while anger is abundant and expensive. Never forget that, in me, you shall always have a brother, no matter where our souls reside. Never stop reaching for success and you will inch your way towards life's best. I love you Retha.

My brother, Terry, at a very young age you were forced to not only be my brother, but in some cases my father as well. Though we rarely spoke, I listened as you talked to others. We seldom conversed over the matters of life, and I learned that spoken words are many times over rated. I never told you this, but as a child you were my hero. I love you Fly.

My uncle, James, it has always been the degree of love inside your heart that really mattered the most. The memories we've shared are priceless. I love you as if you were my very own father and I will never stop needing you, nor will I ever quit trying to become a better person in your eyes.

L.A., the piece 'Because of You' was written because I love you deeply, my brother. You not only knew how to spell the word 'friend', you loved me by its premise. I could have never written this book without your love and support, my dearest and closest friend. Thank you for allowing me to see life through your eyes until I was able to see it through my own.

To my co-workers at 'Simply Unique,' thanks a million for allowing me to pass out my pieces to your clients. I love you all for making me feel like a brother and for filling my heart with so much love. My soul has been truly blessed by the spirit that lives inside our home away from home. To each station I send my deepest and truest affection with love always from me, Doc, your brother for life.

To my Grandmother, thank you for every moment you have spent down on your knees and for every time you've taken a break out of your life to listen.

Wallace, my stepfather, thank you for standing in a gap that very few men before you dared. I know you are a good man; my spirit tells me so.

To my father, I shall continue to wait in the middle of the road so that we might one day make it right. Reconciliation has always been a dream of mine.

My cousin, Sam, our conversations have always been a blessing to me, but none of them touched me more than the day you said you'd be my brother. I shall always love you for that. Thanks a million for being you.

Bobby T. and Leon, man where would I be without the wisdom you two guys possess. I love you brothers for mentally getting at me and for running with me through this marathon of emotional madness. Much love and props go out to you.

T.O., first of all thanks for supporting my dream. I believe that true friends have a way of making themselves visible, even in the darkest of times. I believe that true friends are appointed by God, not merely chosen by man. I will be here when all of the lights have gone out and the fans have gone home. In time, I pray that God will show you, my brother, that I am the uncut rendition of his truths.

To Gwen McDonald, Carlos Watson, Keena Turner, Naomi Kai Kor, and the rest of the 49ERS who helped manifest this book's existence, I thank you. In one way or another, you all have played an instrumental role in what is now a reality for me. I thank you from the depths of my soul.

To the rest of my entire family, I pray that my writing this book makes you proud, but more than anything else, may it remind you that nothing is impossible if you believe in who you are. Remain encouraged and remember that nothing good comes from anger and nothing sweet comes from bitterness. Be better than your worst enemy and stronger than your weakest moment. Writing has opened doors that were at one time barricaded. My diligence and your support have paved the way to success. Achieving my goals is but one part of the struggle, maintaining my relationship with those that love me is the other.

To Tino, Toynes, Victor, Barry, Graves, Damon "DC" Crow, Crieg, "Lil' Mozell", Moe, Phil, Ron "The Wizard" Ward, Royce, Mike "D", Mike Taylor, and Terrance, thank you all for sharing your mental gifts and allowing me to feel the support true friends bestow.

To Bridget DuRuz, thanks for your editing.

There will be names that may not be mentioned, but believe me when I say that I love each and every one of you who has played a role in my literal recovery. Please know that you are loved.

This book is to 'Keeping It Real.'

Foreword
"Why I Write"

One day while I was in my darkest state of mind, I finally turned off the TV and for the first time commenced keeping my ears close to readers: as close as possible. By doing so, I began to grow. Not everyone will make it out of the dark world from which I have traveled, but hopefully my voice will be able to shine some light on the many souls of this world that have gone unheard. Though it is true I walked this earth for years without the use of words, my greatest victory comes through my being able to walk humbly with translating facts of truths. Since becoming literate, I have written many stories, but none of them are greater than my own.

For so many years my voice has been silenced, and today I am excited to speak. If not for myself, then for those who I have promised to remember. As I speak on miscellaneous matters of life, I will do my best not to veer away from the truth. I have learned that through listening to others, we can create a thruway that will link us to an emotional truth. So today, I write in an attempt to reach deeper into myself; to pass those self-imposed intuitions, which have led so many men to make inaccurate conclusions. I feel that a writer must allow his soul to succumb to the facts, instead of submitting to his own personal views. When life had gotten too dark for me to see, I simply closed my eyes and allowed my soul to lead me.

So many of us aren't willing to accept the truth, so we attempt to manufacture our own. No one has the power to change what is, no more than we have the power to undo what was. Although at times I might sound as if I am clairvoyant, believe me when I say that I am not unaware of my limitations. I have learned to never set my goals higher than I am willing to soar. I will never stop learning, no matter how many awards of accomplishment I receive. So if life's dark cloud begins to hover again, I will continue to press forward.

If I'm never given another opportunity to place my mental impressions on paper, let me say that I am overwhelmed and deeply humbled at this very moment. No matter what happens after you finish reading my work, I will never stop writing. Not even if all forms of pencil and paper are destroyed. I will write upon the walls of my soul before I allow this world to place me back into an illiterate state of mind.

> In 1974, a teacher told a young boy,
> while in grade school, that he would never
> be able to function in life as a normal person.
> Every time he heard that shameful lie,
> he lifted his soul up to the sky.
> He cried out many times through the night,
> asking God why he was chosen

to carry such a plight.
Through his prayers he was given
the strength to carry on
and because of his diligence
he now sits upon a throne.
Those who cannot read yet still dare to believe,
should listen to Him when He says that
you too can achieve.
For no one should have to live a lifetime
without having the access to words.
For the understanding of words,
many times, is the ruler by which we are measured.
I am merely an instrument that needed
to be played by the game of life.
I do hope that you enjoy the way my
soul strokes the keys.
For my wish is to somehow invite
you inside a mind that was once illiterate.

TABLE OF CONTENTS

"Shattered Lives"

An Illegitimate Child
17

What Ever Happened To Forever
49

Four Boys And A Girl
147

Our Children Are Watching Us
169

Nicoli Is My Name
211

An Illegitimate Child

I am the illegitimate child of two fools, born out of lust and raised by any means necessary. My mother was the town whore and my daddy was the biggest damn dog to ever walk on two legs. It was told to me that they met one day while indulging in their social occupations. After several drinks and a lot of shit talking I was conceived in the back of an old 1957 Chevy, which apparently was deserted by someone who had either run out of money, time, or patience. My daddy's nickname was *Quick* and my mama's was *LayLay*. My guess is that I was probably the result of four or fives strokes, my trifling mama only being on her back long enough to open up her legs and reach out for a sorry ass nigga, who had no doubt already come and gone.

My mother had very limited time for nurturing. She abandoned me just a few days before her seventeenth birthday. I've been told that she stopped by the liquor store early that day to cash her welfare check. After doing so she placed a card inside my carriage that read, "Baby, I'm sorry that I couldn't raise you. I love you dearly, and I hope you have a great life." Oh yes, I almost forgot, she left me five dollars and some change.

She placed me in front of the local hospital where I was found a few hours later. Since that day I've been in and out of five foster homes. I've been physically abused, beat on, and laid on, by some of this world's sleaziest.

I really don't know what I hated most, being in a foster home or being appraised for one. Having to come out in a single-file-line, to turn around and raise my arms was humiliating. I guess that was when they counted to make sure we had all our fingers. Each one of us had to open our mouths, lift up our feet and hands, just like slaves in an auction. This was so degrading and we all hated it, but it had to be done, as prospective foster parents looked us over.

Though my first four years of life were spent inside the walls of discouragement, I didn't know to be unhappy. Up to that point I had no real place to call my home, but I wore an amazing smile and had a captivating personality. I was what the children's shelter called 'a keeper.' The people there would often refer to me as being a joy to have around, a flower of life and a blessing from heaven.

I was about four and a half years old when a Caucasian couple out of Chicago came to rescue and adopt me. They were two people looking for someone to love, someone to care for, and I just happened to be available. A little black girl named Kenisha...from Cleveland. Who would have guessed it? I was that missing piece of their puzzle, their little bundle of joy. When I first met Mr. and Mrs. Dan and Julie Bradley, I was taken by their warmth. They were both in their mid-to-late thirties and had nothing but love to give. It was a foster child's dream come true.

We lived in a three-bedroom, two-car garage home, with fancy furniture and every extra anyone could imagine. Mr. Dan came from 'old money' as Mrs. Julie put it. He was used to the finer things in life and made sure she had it all. She didn't appear to take it for granted, and at times seemed more excited about being there than I was.

Mr. Dan was an insurance salesman who wasn't really good at selling much of anything. But he didn't have to be. His parents had left him more than enough money to live on for the rest of his life. At least that's what I overheard Mrs. Julie tell her friends over the telephone. Mr. Dan was an attractive man who stood about five-nine and weighed about 180 pounds. He had blond hair and wore it neatly cut. He was a suit-wearing man but didn't particularly like wearing ties. Mrs. Julie insisted on it though. When he refused to wear one, she'd walk over to him and whisper something in his ear. Whatever she told him placed a smile on his face and made him feel better about wearing that tie. Mr. Dan loved his wife deeply and wanted her to be happy more than anything. I think that's why he brought her to Cleveland to adopt me.

Mrs. Julie was a housewife who loved cooking and cleaning. She kept the house in tip-top shape. She was a tall woman with a beautiful body that drove Mr. Dan wild. Her deep brown hair had an amazing shine to it. Sometimes she'd let me brush it as she closed her eyes and lay in bed next to me. Her lovely skin looked like she polished it daily. But it was her genuine love that drew me to her. I guess it was that same love that brought her and Mr. Dan together.

After two blissful years had passed, I started to notice that something was different. I sensed a bit of frustration in the air. A spirit came to visit our home and I knew something was going terribly wrong. While setting the dinner table one night, the spirit got the better of me.

"Kenisha, what's wrong?" Mrs. Julie asked.

I didn't want to complain. I was taught in the shelter to deal with whatever the moment brings. I knew that crybabies were sent back. I didn't want to go back. I wanted to stay with my new family. So I just sat there, trying to hold my peace, hoping I wouldn't have to answer the question.

"Kenisha, what's wrong?" Mr. Dan asked in a concerned tone.

"Nothing. I'm just not feeling well," I finally replied. But the spirit won and I began to cry.

Mrs. Julie jumped up from her seat and rushed over to hug me. "Please, Baby, tell me what's wrong," she insisted.

She was hugging me so tight I could feel her chest trembling.

"I need to know what's wrong with you."

"I made you mad and now you don't love me anymore," I sadly replied.

"Oh, no... That's not true, Kenisha. We love you so. We never stopped loving you. You've done nothing wrong."

Mr. Dan continued, "We were going to talk to you about it when we felt you were old enough to understand."

"Old enough to understand what t? Are you talking about the spirit?"

"What spirit?" asked Mrs. Julie.

"The spirit that makes everybody sad."

"Kenisha, Baby, there are some things in life we have no control of. One of those things is death. A long time ago Mrs. Julie and I found out that she was very sick. We were first told that the cancer she had could be fixed. But now they say it can't."

Over the past two years I often heard Mr. Dan attempting to comfort Mrs. Julie, but I didn't think much of it. Now it all began to make sense to me. I understood why I'd seen Mrs. Julie bending over holding her side. Now I knew I was sensing was the cancer. The evil spirit was cancer. It had gotten into Mrs. Julie and made her sick

She had always been so upbeat, so warm and sure of herself. She was full of life and such a joy to be around. She made me laugh sometimes until I cried. She would count to ten and tell me to hide, and within minutes find me. Then she'd pick me up, throw me over her shoulder, and race around the house with me. She was my lifeline of nurturing, my warm place to snuggle when my world got cold. I began thinking about how I would miss her combing my hair and putting pretty ribbons all over my head. She taught me that no matter what people said about me, I was beautiful. She made me believe I was special and that's all there was to it. The thought of God taking her from me made me angry. He knew that she was all I had. He knew she was my only source of reasoning.

It gave me comfort to know they weren't mad at me. But the fact that Mrs. Julie wasn't going to be around much longer was devastating. I needed God to explain to me why He was taking away the only other woman in my life. This special woman who I hoped would support me in my efforts to become a woman. Why wouldn't I be given a chance to know either of them long enough to make a real difference in my life?

Mrs. Julie was truly a fighter, but not even she could defeat this spirit. She lived for another six or seven months before God finally came and closed her eyes. After her death, Mr. Dan lost his will to go on and was committed to a psychiatric hospital. Then I was returned to the children's shelter in Cleveland of course.

I was almost ten when I went into my second placement. Miss Jackson, the foster home placement supervisor, had me waiting by the front door when Miss McFarland came to get me on a cold, rainy afternoon. I was told me she was a tall woman, but when she walked in she was more like a giant! She was a mangy looking white woman who towered over us all, and her six-foot plus frame was built like five days of bad weather. Her piercing eyes emphasized the anger written all over her face. Her motives for adopting me were as evident as the slight limp in her walk. Her hair was red as fire and her smile was cold as her hatred towards her foster children. She was forty-two, but looked fifty-two.

We had heard in the home that there were people out there who took foster children for the money. Miss McFarland had 'pay me' written all over her face. Miss

Jackson would not have let me go with that woman, but was with another placement, and her assistant tried to sell Miss McFarland on choosing me.

When our eyes met she pointed directly at me and asked in a stern voice, "Is that her? Well, if that's all you have, I guess she'll have to do. I was expecting her to be stronger looking."

"She's a very clean young lady and gets along well with others. We've never had any problems with her and I'm sure you'll like her." She turned to me and said, "Kenisha, go with this nice lady. You listen to her and be good now, you hear?"

When we arrived at Miss McFarland's house I met her three adopted children. I soon realized this family had its own set of problems and I didn't see why they needed to include me. No one in the family seemed to like each other. I could tell right from the start I wouldn't like it there either. I kept to myself whenever I could.

Lisa, my roommate, was about seven. She was almost as tall as me, but was as round as a twenty-five inch TV. She was quiet but had a mean spirit in her eyes.

Five-year old Randy was the child from hell. I would put my life on it. Something was seriously wrong with Randy. HeHHh was constantly digging in his nose. Whenever someone looked at him, he would stick the same finger in his mouth, laughing loudly like he had just discovered a new flavor of ice cream. Maybe he just needed a friend.

Last but surely not least, was Andrew. He was the oldest at seventeen. He was not really a bad guy; he just couldn't keep his damn hands to himself. Andrew had gotten a hold of some Playboy magazines and was losing his mind. I think that he had a thing for chocolate, because all he ever talked about was getting his hands on me.

Even at home Miss McFarland continued to be mad at the world. She was also lazy and nasty, the two worst traits I was told a woman could have. She would beat her kids for no reason. I was not there twenty-four hours before she attempted to beat me.

"Come here, come here," she would demand. "You belong to me now and you will do what I say. You hear?"

I didn't mean anything by my simple answer, but it sent me back to the foster home. While looking Miss McFarland straight in her eyes I stated, "You don't have to beat me for no reason. I am a good child and I will obey your rules."

This angered Miss McFarland, who slapped me upside the head and yelled, "No child talks to me that way. Not in my house! If you don't like it here, I'll take you back. Hell, I can get six hundred dollars for keeping anyone of you little pieces of dirt."

After being yelled at, I ran back into the room I shared with Lisa. She was laughing at me because I had been slapped by the wicked evil witch of Cleveland. Shouting, "Shut-up!" silenced her, but I was so fed up I grabbed my bags and sat them down near the front door.

Little Randy ran over to me and said, "Please don't go, I like you."

I could feel his sincerity but I couldn't stay. Andrew asked me to stay, but he had ulterior motives. The nasty little bugger was just thinking about himself. Lisa had nothing to say.

Miss McFarland took me back to the children's shelter where I stayed for about two and a half more years.

I was twelve years old before going into my third home. I'll never forget how strange I felt from the first moment I laid eyes on the new couple. The Normans complimented me on the length of my hair. It was jet black and stopped mid way down my back. I was pretty now, and I knew it. The little boys told me all the time. I was filling out in places that I never thought I would.

Mrs. Jackson would always say, "Child you'd best be careful. You are maturing much too fast for your age, and little boys are going to start looking at you in a funny kind of way." She smiled as she often times did. I knew what she was talking about.

Mrs. Norman had previously come to the placement home inquiring about me several times. Mrs. Jackson felt that the Normans and I made a nice match and I was running out of time. You see, when foster children reach their teens it gets harder and harder to find placement.

Mrs. Jackson introduced me to the Normans. "This is Kenisha, one of our prized loved ones. She cooks and cleans well. She's not a lot of trouble. Kenisha just needs a loving home and a brand new start. You see, she suffers from a broken heart."

"Oh, we feel we have just the place for her," said Mr. Norman with a sinister smile.

"Well, everything checked out and she's yours," Mrs. Jackson stated.

I bet I had heard that a hundred times or more and each time it left a bad taste in my mouth. It sometimes meant there was trouble ahead, and stories of foster children being abused were told on a regular basis. I was not getting any younger, and going with them provided me with a place to live. My need to be placed into a home was greater than my fear of being molested. I had to believe that God would protect me from all that was evil.

I remember leaving the children's shelter wearing a blue dress; one that had been given to me a year ago by a friend who had died from we called 'a lonely spirit.' I put what few belongings I had in the trunk of the Norman's car. I got inside the car remembering to keep my dress pulled down towards my knees. All the horror stories I had heard about molestation suddenly buzzed into my mind. We were barely out of the parking lot when the madness began. I will never forget how Mr. Norman leered at me through the rearview mirror, all the while pretending to adjust it. I could feel his eyes pierce my panties and roam across my chest. His eyes, an odd shade of blue, were attempting to look between my legs at what the shelter's group workers had taught all the young girls was our special place. A place I called my 'kitty cat.'

Mr. Norman was a nasty old bastard with crooked teeth. He had a funny little mustache and a scar on the left side of his face that was noticeable from a distance. The drive to their home took over an hour, but felt like days. Mr. Norman had a lot to say to his wife, and every now and then he actually said something that made sense. Mrs. Norman hardly said a word.

We were about halfway there when Mr. Norman stared back through the mirror and spoke directly to me. "Kenisha, I hope you're going to like living with us. We've always wanted a little girl, but my wife can't have kids." Mr. Norman seemed to control every conversation.

I learned he was an investment banker who had done well for himself over the years. Their house showed off his financial success. It was two stories with eight or nine rooms and there was a basement, which I was told was off limits. Later I would come to know why. My room was beautiful, and was furnished with everything a girl could ask for.

Mr. Norman said, "I do a lot of my studying down in the basement. No one is allowed down there, no one."

Mrs. Norman spoke softly, "Don't feel bad, Baby, he never allows me down there either."

I promised to stay out of the basement.

Mrs. Norman was a housewife who spent her time playing bridge, decorating the house and shopping for clothes. She was a tall, slender lady and not hard to look at. The clothes she wore were gorgeous. She took me shopping almost every weekend. She loved to buy pretty undergarments and always insisted that I get some for myself.

"But Mrs. Norman, you've already bought me over twenty pairs."

"Baby," she said, "you can never have too many pairs of undergarments."

I barely saw Mr. Norman and that was all right with me, but one night after dinner, Mr. Norman complimented me on a new dress that I was wearing. "Kenisha, that is a lovely dress," he said in an eerie tone, which made me very uncomfortable.

At the end of August when school was to start soon, Mr. Norman stated, "Mrs. Norman and I have decided to send you to a private school on the other side of town. We hope you will like it there."

"I'm sure I will, Mr. Norman," I said with a smile. "Thank you for the opportunity." I did indeed feel very grateful.

That night while getting undressed I thought I heard a strange moaning sound. But I thought it must be my imagination. The Normans' bedroom was all the way down at the end of the hall, and no one else was in the house.

I continued to take off the rest of my clothes and put on my robe. I went to the bathroom, midway down the hall, to take a shower. I loved smelling fresh when I laid down for sleep at night. I sat down on the toilet to groom the hair that surrounded my 'kitty cat.' I heard that sound again, but this time it seemed a lot closer to the Normans' bedroom.

The sound of a car outside startled me, so I rushed over to the window. Much to my surprise Mrs. Norman was pulling up in the driveway. Seeing her by herself I did not really know what to think. Was I going crazy? Now I knew that I was not imagining things. There was moaning coming from somewhere. I hurried and jumped into the shower, cleaning myself as fast as I could.

When I came out of the bathroom Mr. Norman was standing there, smiling at me as if I were one of his largest bank investments ever.

"Good-night pretty girl. Sleep tight, don't let the bed bugs bite," he said with a crazy look in his eyes. That confirmed it. I was not losing my mind. I had always prided myself on my ability to hear well. I heard things that many times were not meant for my ears.

There was a knock at my door. "Come in," I said reluctantly.

It was Mrs. Norman asking me to start cleaning up better after myself. Her request surprised me as I had cleaned up religiously in the shelter for years and had shared a room with at least ten other children at times. Any thought of returning to the shelter made me feel sick inside. So the next morning I decided that never again would anyone in the Norman's household have reason to question my ability to clean up after myself. I remember getting up early, straightening every inch of my room in such a way that my cleanliness would never come into question.

I could not wait until everyone left the house for the day. Mr. Norman left early, around six, and usually arrived home around dinnertime. Mrs. Norman usually spent the mornings shopping then played bridge with some of the other wealthy ladies in the neighborhood at noon each day. She'd be gone for five or six hours. That would be long enough for me to make a lasting impression on the Normans. I started on the main floor, cleaning every nook and cranny. Returning to the children's shelter was not going to be because I wasn't clean enough.

My efforts were paying off and everything was going well, until I started cleaning up the Normans' room. It was a large room with elaborate furniture. I started to straighten up the bed. The texture of the bed was quite extravagant. There seemed to be enough silk on their bed to clothe a small orphanage. Little did I know that I was about to embark upon a secret that would keep me in emotional bondage and ultimately lead me back to the shelter.

After making up the bed, I gathered up the business cards and other literature that was sitting near the nightstand. Much to my surprise, there were many photos of me inside an envelope. It also contained a large key, which I carelessly placed on top of the nightstand.

Many of the pictures were taken of me while I was in my room naked, preparing for bed or getting ready to put on my undergarments. My feelings were hurt, crushed into what felt like a million small pieces. It seemed like what a rape victim must feel. I wanted to tell someone, but I had no one to talk to. I was not allowed to have any friends until I had shown that I could do well in school. I thought that I ought to tell Mrs. Norman, but something told me she already knew. The real reason for all of those trips to the mall had started to sink in and what I felt as genuine love for my well being, was all just one great big lie.

I sat down on the edge of the bed with my face buried in the palms of my hands. I cried like I did when I was told that my birth mother had abandoned me. "Oh God, where are you now? Have you forsaken me, or is this just a dream?"

I heard the front door closing and began to panic. There were pictures of me scattered all over the bed. I needed to pull myself together and scrambled to put away my devastating discovery. The Normans had hardwood floors throughout their home, which made it easy to hear anyone coming or going. My heart was beating faster than ever as I heard approaching footsteps. My time was running out. There were two more pictures just out of reach when the bedroom door opened. It was Mr. Norman. I later learned he had taken the day off to spend with Mrs. Norman.

"What is that in your hand?" he asked in a very stern voice.

I was scared to death. What was I going to say? I bit my tongue and said nothing at all. I tried to place the pictures behind my back.

"What is that in your hands?" he demanded as he turned to lock the door. I quickly reached for the key that I had placed on the nightstand and put it into my pocket.

"Kenisha, you haven't been looking through my things now have you?"

"No sir, Mr. Norman, no sir!"

"Then please tell me what it is that you're holding behind your back."

By that time, I could tell he already knew I had seen the pictures.

"Kenisha," he announced plainly, "this world is full of sick people and I just happen to be one of them. I have always been fascinated by the skin color of black people and my wife knows it."

He stared coldly at the shocked look on my face and continued, "Yes, that's right. Mrs. Norman finds me little girls like you in return for a life of luxury. All I really want to do is watch," he said taking small steps towards me. He placed his right hand upon my cheek and attempted to rub it. I moved my face away from his touch. I could feel him growing angry.

"Well, you ungrateful little bitch. I gave you a place to stay, and this is the thanks I get!"

He grabbed both of my arms and pushed me onto the bed. He shouted, "The last little tramp Mrs. Norman brought into my home put this scar on my face! Can't you see that being here is better than living in some foster home?"

"N-n-o," I stammered, and tried to crawl to the end of the bed.

"Where in the hell do you think you're going?"

"Mr. Norman. Please, please don't hurt me. Please!" I begged. With both of his hands he pulled on the front part of my blouse and the buttons began to fly across the room while he ripped it apart. He did the same thing with my bra.

I swung at him for the first time, wildly trying to release his grip on me. I'd been told that a man's private area was very tender, and if all else failed I was to kick them there as hard as I possibly could. I mustered up my strength and kicked. He tumbled over on his side holding himself. A deep grimace developed on his face. I unlocked the door as ran as fast as I could to hide.

Mr. Norman was hollering, "Come back here you little black bitch! Come back here!"

I could hear him coming after me. He was moving faster than I was, and the smell of his bad breath was growing near.

"Kenisha, I'm not going to hurt you, just come out from wherever you are and let me talk to you!" he shouted.

I thought, I may be young, I may be black, and at any time now I might be a foster child again, but there's one thing for sure, I ain't no fool. I was running out of places to hide when it dawned on me, I was sure I had the key to the basement in my pocket. I took off my shoes and crept slowly down the stairs.

I ran through the kitchen and opened the back door to make it look like I ran out of the house. I moved quickly to place the large key in the basement door. I remembered to lock it behind me as I crept down the dark stairs. I could hear Mr. Norman leave the house through the back door as I sat down in a small room to collect my thoughts. At first, it was dark, but by the time my eyes focused, I could see some light coming from a tiny hole in the middle of the wall. I stood up to inspect it. To my surprise, I could somehow see into the upstairs bathroom. The same bathroom I used to shower in every night. I felt total disgust. This is where the sounds had been coming from. Mr. Norman had been watching me, and God only knew who else, through the periscope system he had fashioned in the wall.

I walked out of the room into the hallway and noticed small rooms throughout the basement. There was a photographer's darkroom where he developed his sick pictures. On the wall, were photos of ten or fifteen girls, but what saddened me most was that they all seemed younger than me. There was a camera set up in another room farther down the hall. I thought it must be connected to my room, but I wasn't willing to waste my time finding out. Breathing became harder as a million questions began to run through my head. What had I done to God that would have made him place me in such a horrible situation?

I wasn't ready to go back to the children's shelter, but I knew that I had to get out of there. As I reached the top of the steps, I heard Mrs. Norman walk through the front door and upstairs.

"Kenisha!" she yelled. "Where are you, Baby?"

I wasn't scared of her. I stepped into the kitchen, closing the basement door softly. "Here I am Mrs. Norman. Here I am," I called to her from the foot of the stairs.

She was coming out of my bedroom with some of my things in her hand.

"I want you to take a ride with me," she said as she walked down the stairs.

I knew where she was taking me, but I played along with her, and got in the car.

"I want to take you to get some ice cream but first there is some more paper work we have to fill out over at the shelter. Don't worry, this won't take long."

"Have you talked to Mr. Norman today?" I asked while she concentrated on the road.

"No dear, I haven't," she replied. Her flat tone indicated she was lying.

When we pulled into the parking lot, I knew that this would be the last time we would ever see each other. We got out of the car, and went inside where Mrs. Jackson was waiting. She grabbed my hand, and led me back to my old room.

As I looked back over my shoulder I said, "Hey, Mrs. Norman, thanks for the ice cream and, oh yes, the undergarments as well."

I was sad that yet another placement had not worked out, but not as sad as I was for those other girls who had come before me. I neglected to tell Mrs. Jackson about the terrible things that had happened to me at the Normans. My complaint might make her think twice about finding me new placement. There were many kids who had become hard to place. I did not want to be put on that list. What had happened to me was wrong, but I would get over it.

After a while, wrong becomes just like the weather. It has no other choice but to change. I learned at an early age that peace belongs to no one, but rather it is a cloud that hovers over us like the seasons. If it were not for summer, how could we truly enjoy the fall? I began to read my Bible, and pray for the clouds of misery to drift away, and allow the sun of elation to dawn on my heart with its smile. I had to believe that all the things that had transpired were a test of my faith. If I were to succeed, I had to continue to pass these difficult tests.

As many of the children continued being placed I never lost hope. Hope became my only friend. Every Tuesday night, I'd lie in my bed, listening to the winds blow against the window. I'd cry myself to sleep, while at the same time caressing hope, my only true friend. I cried because I knew that on Wednesday morning another line up would take place and someone very dear to me would probably be leaving. I tried not to look my age, by wearing two ponytails in my hair. I stood in such a way that I looked shorter than I actually was. And, oh yes, I smiled a little extra to enhance my beauty. This routine went on for almost two more years, week in and week out.

I became an aide around the shelter. I was then the oldest girl at age fifteen. My job was to make sure everyone knew the rules and followed them. After all, I knew the place like the back of my hand. Mrs. Jackson felt sorry for me. I could tell by the way she carried on. She always said, "Child if I could, I'd take you home with me."

Nearly a year later, one day before leaving to go home to her husband and four kids, she took me in her arms. She held me as if I were her own. For that brief moment, I felt as if she was my very own mother. After hugging me she grabbed her bags and hurried out the door. Fighting back her tears, she said, "I love you Kenisha."

"I love you too Mrs. Jackson. Have a nice weekend," I managed to whisper.

"I'll see you later Kenisha. Be sweet now, you hear?"

Two days later, on a Monday morning, I was awakened from a deep sleep, and led into the meeting room. It was where we usually went to be reprimanded. I wiped the sleep from my eyes and braced myself for what was to come. Mrs. Jackson motioned to me from an adjoining room. I closed the door behind myself, and nervously asked, "Mrs. Jackson, what have I done wrong?"

"Nothing child, you've done nothing wrong at all. I just have a big surprise for you. So put these clothes on and come to the meeting room at once."

I dressed as fast as I could and rushed to open the door. A man greeted me with a smile, as if I were the missing piece to a million dollar puzzle. I smiled back at him in spite of myself. Here I go again I thought.

I had just turned sixteen and needed a placement like a blind man needs his Seeing Eye dog. I was afraid of the idea of another man wanting to get some of my 'kitty cat,' but even more afraid of living in this world without love.

"Kenisha, say 'hello' to the man," Mrs. Jackson said.

"Hello, sir," I said with a smile. I flashed that same old smile I had smiled over a thousand times.

"Hello, young lady, my name is Mr. Williams. I am a friend of Miss Owens."

I wondered who in the world Miss Owens could be. As Mr. Williams introduced himself to me, one of the most beautiful black women I had ever seen floated through the front door.

"Hello, Sweetie, I'm Miss Owens, your new mother."

I thought it all was a joke, so I played along. "Hello, I am Kenisha, your new daughter."

Miss Owens smiled at me as a delicate tear from her right eye began to slide down her beautiful face. I learned that Miss Owens was a very successful woman who had a deep desire to reach back and try to help someone in need. I couldn't understand why she wanted me when there were so many other younger children. I guess she didn't want a child younger than myself. Perhaps she didn't have time to raise a baby. But whatever the reason, I was more than happy to be chosen. My lucky day had come.

Miss Owens began to speak, "I've seen so many pictures of you and I'm so glad to finally meet you."

I had longed to hear those words, and could hardly believe my ears hearing them for the first time. With my heart fluttering from the thought of hearing more, I turned towards Mrs. Jackson for confirmation. Through her tears, I understood my dreams of one day having someone truly love me had become a reality. My new mother didn't want to own me, she didn't want a slave, she wanted me. Finally, a part of me was free.

Miss Owens said, "Sweetie, you look great in your new clothes. Do you like them?"

Miss Owens had bought the clothes that I had put on, but I failed to notice my attire due to the rush. Looking at them for the first time I replied, "I love them. They are so beautiful, just like you."

Mrs. Jackson was wiping away tears of joy as she walked with us towards the car. I turned and said to her, "I will miss you Mrs. Jackson."

"I know, I will miss you too," she said in her softest voice.

Miss Owens' long time friend, Mr. Williams, had taken the drive to witness her fulfill her dreams of one day having a child of her own. I later came to know him as Stan. He took my bags to the car, saying to me, "Kenisha, you don't have to carry anything heavy again." I noticed Mr. Williams standing on the car's right side. He opened Miss Owens' door and closed it behind her.

I smiled and thought how nice that was to see. As I reached for the back door, much to my surprise, he opened my door as well.

"God," I muttered, "if this is another of your tricks, I'll kill you." My intense jubilation produced a smile my face that hurt my cheeks!

"Kenisha," Miss Owens said. "I'm sorry I missed my two appointments to meet with you before, but my mother has been sick and she's just starting to feel better."

I never knew anything about missed meetings. I was just glad that she had come to take me now. She lived on 'the other side of town,' in an apartment building that was bigger than anything I had ever seen.

"Is this where you live Miss Owens?"

"No, this is where we live. This is our home."

"We. Yes, that's right."

The apartment was on the fifth floor with a spectacular view of the city. When she opened up the door, there were beautiful pictures everywhere. My room overwhelmed me. I had my own TV, a telephone and a stereo. I even had two beds. Miss Owens said they were in case one of my friends wanted to come over and spend the night.

"Miss Owens?"

"What is it, Sweetie?"

"It took me sixteen years to get my own room and I'm not ready to share it with anyone just yet."

"Okay, Sweetie, you don't have to if you don't want to. Here are your keys for the apartment. Now this key fits the laundry room, which is located downstairs near the elevators." She barely stopped to take a breath. "I don't have as many rules as you had in the children's shelter, but I do have some do's and don'ts. I want to go over them with you tomorrow, before I go back to work."

"That's fine with me Miss Owens. Whatever you say."

Early the next morning, around eight o'clock there was a knock at the door.

"Come in," I said. It was Miss Owens.

"Kenisha, may I come in and sit with you for a moment?"

I understood I had a twisted view of some aspects of life, and just the fact that she asked my permission really shook me up. "Miss Owens, this is your house, what right do I have to say yes or no to you?"

"Sweetie, this is your room," she said leaning towards me, "and these are your keys. I don't know what you are accustomed to, but in my world everyone has rights." I couldn't stop smiling as she continued, "I took the liberty of throwing away those bags you had. You won't be needing them any longer."

For the better part of my life, I had kept my bags partially packed, knowing that at any time I might have to go back to the home.

"Sweetie, what's wrong? Did I say something wrong?"

"No, Miss Owens. It's just all happening so fast. I don't know how to react is all."

"Then why are you crying?"

"These are not tears of sorrow. These are tears of joy. The reason there are so many is I have never cried these tears before."

From that day forward, my life took on a new direction. Miss Owens, whom I later began to call Mama, became my mentor in life. She was an ambitious, strong black woman, who taught me to be strong. She taught me how to mimic her ways, by constantly displaying a fight I had never before seen in a woman. Her pure love for me was special. Her desire for me to overcome life's trials was second to her strong admiration for me as she watched me succeed in my endeavors. She was the epitome of all that was beautiful, and she inspired me with her spirit.

I was almost forty years old when I came to know who my real mother was. Miss Owens was in her sixties and had been retired for almost seven years when I began to ask her about my past. I visited her one day on the way home from work to share the troubles of my soul. She knew I needed to find closure for this life long mystery. Miss Owens wasn't at all upset, in fact, she seemed to be prepared for what I was asking.

"Everyone needs to know where they come from and it's about time you learned who your real parents are."

"Mama, as far as I am concerned you are my real mother."

"Yes, I know, Sweetie. That will never change. But we all need to know where we come from."

"Mama, are you mad that I'm asking?"

"No, I thought you'd ask sooner though, but I never wanted it to be a secret. I've always wanted you to have the very best that life has to offer." She gave me a folder that had my parents' names and addresses on it. She'd kept the information updated over the years and had stored it in a safe place.

"Child, your father died about four years ago from lung cancer. He was a corner salesman who ran out of things to sell. He was never told anything about you. When you were born he was in prison. Two years later, by the time he saw your mother again, she was twenty years old. Not once did she ever mention to him that he had fathered a child."

The need to see my mother enveloped me. So I took some time off and traveled back to Cleveland. I was told my mother had been living there since my birth. I called her number from a phone booth at the airport, only to find out she had recently been admitted into the local hospital. She was only fifty-seven years old and on her deathbed in need of a blood transfusion.

At the hospital I was told she was in the critical care unit. I really didn't care what condition she was in. That's not why I was there. I just wanted to see the woman who had abandoned me over thirty-nine years ago. I had a need to see her face and for her to see mine. When I reached her floor, I asked for Miss Wanda Dixon, a.k.a. *LayLay,* at the information desk. I was told that only immediate family members could have access to the type of information I was seeking.

"Oh, you see, I am her daughter."

The nurse looked at me as if I was a ghost. She asked, "Are you sure?"

"Yes, why do you ask 'am I sure?' "

"Well, I've already contacted the rest of her family about any more next of kin. Why didn't anyone tell me that Miss Dixon had a daughter? We are looking for a type of O positive blood, which very few people in this world are able to match."

I had found out years ago that my blood type was rare. It immediately occurred to me that I probably was a match.

"Are you willing to give blood to save Miss Dixon's life?"

What in the hell was I doing here in this hospital? The same place I was abandoned years ago. My mind was spinning.

"Her condition is fading fast and since you are her daughter, maybe you'll be able to save her life."

"No, that is not why I'm here."

The nurse responded by saying, "Wait just one minute, while I notify the rest of the family that you've arrived."

About two minutes later the nurse returned with an elderly woman. I could tell that she was looking for me because the nurse was pointing in my direction.

She came over to me and said, "Oh, my Lord. It's you. Wanda told me that she had a child but I never got a chance to see you. I was living in another state, and by the time I found out about you, she had already given up her rights."

The old woman was my grandmother. For years I had wondered just where I had gotten my beautiful eyes, and now after all this time I could see that the eyes that were glowing from her head were the same as mine.

"Baby, I have prayed that you'd come, for over a month now. Please tell me that you will give your blood to save your mother's life."

"Look, whoever you are. I don't know you and anyway, why should I give a damn whether this person that you call my mother lives or dies?"

The old woman began to cry. "Then why are you here?" she said through her tears.

I stood there speechless, reaching for the words to express my emotions. "Miss, this is not against you, but my mother left me to die and did not love me enough to raise me."

She replied, "Baby, she wasn't stable enough to raise you herself. But she cared enough to take you to the hospital and leave you where you could be found. For years she carried around an enormous amount of pain inside her heart. She never forgot you. I have held her in my arms a million times and wiped away her tears. I can honestly say that she loves you dearly."

She hesitated then asked me once more, "Why did you come here? Why are you here?"

"I came here to see the woman who gave birth to me and left me out in the cold to die."

"No, Baby," she replied, as she took me by my hand and led me towards the elevators. She pressed the button to the bottom floor. We walked out the side door of the hospital. She stopped near the doorway and pointed. "This is where your mother left you." She was pointing to a large oak tree across the grass.

"Baby, do you see those flowers underneath that old tree? Your mother has placed them there once a week, as far back as I can remember. She has not had a great life and I'm sure you haven't either. I understand the sacrifices. You have every right to leave her bedside today. Take some time to think about it. Please remember that you are the only person who can save her life."

With that, she turned and walked back into the hospital, leaving me there to make the same decision my mother had to make over thirty-nine years ago. I walked closer to the tree. As I got nearer, I saw there was something carved into the trunk. It read, 'Oh God, I'm sorry for leaving her here. Please bring her back to me one day.' Here I was standing underneath the same tree where, as an infant, for all intents and purposes I had been left to die. Life now depended upon me.

I lifted my head towards heaven and asked these questions: "God, does this have to happen in order for my life to be manifested? Please tell me, is my blood the same blood that runs through her body? If so, will my donation truly make it right?"

Without even knowing it, my body turned towards the hospital doors. I was on my way back upstairs. I regained my composure and entered the critical care floor once more, still without thinking.

There lay a woman, my mother, beaten down by life, and dragged down by the realities of her transgressions. Her eyes were closed but something told me that she could feel my presence. I cringed as her eyes began to blink. They seemed too weak to open.

I felt the need to tell her I was there. I moved closer hoping she might hear my voice and the sound alone might make her eyes open.

My heart was experiencing a connection, which had for years eluded me. Suddenly I was no longer afraid to speak to her. "Mama, this is me," I said.

A smile appeared on her face and her eyes began to open. She turned to look at me and for the first time in my life I felt whole. "Baby," she asked. "Is that really you?"

"Yes, Mama, it's me," I comforted her.

Her hands reached out to touch my face and my soul began to swallow her pain. Somewhere between pushing through the door and Mama opening up her eyes, my anger dissipated.

"Hook me up!" I shouted to the nurse at the top of my lungs. "Hook me up now!" I was calling for a nurse to come and take my blood.

My grandmother fell to her knees and began to pray to the same God that had protected me over the years. At that very moment, my need to know about my past no longer mattered, but rather God's moment of truth needed to be manifested. He knew one day Wanda, my birth mother, would need me to save her life. He also knew that I would not say no.

My blood matched hers and the transfusion was a success. The next morning Wanda was still weak from all that had taken place, yet she was removed from the critical ward. Two weeks later she was released from the hospital.

I now have a relationship with Wanda. But never can she replace my earthly mother. I spend much of my time talking to Miss Owens over the phone, and she is still the love of my life. I love her for caring enough about me to reconnect me to my roots. But most of all for having enough love inside her heart to share some with me.

I remember calling her after the blood transfusion to explain everything in detail. She was so proud of me that she began to cry. "Baby," she said, "you were born for this day. I'm so happy you made the right decision. God will bless you for what you've done."

"No, Mama. He already did, the day you came into my life. Thank you. All we've done is God's work and that is a beautiful thing. Our life is a testimony of God's grace, our strength is indicative of His glory."

Miss Owens was a proud old woman, who gave like she loved. I will never forget her sweet spirit and the harmony that she injected into my life. She taught me that before our birth, our purpose has already been written. But it is through our choices that we either allow or disallow it to be realized.

My life was not perfect. By no means were we meant to live without struggle. Success without some type of adversity is almost unheard of. So, I no longer find myself asking why my feet had to be placed on the path of despair. God knew that my life would heal the lives of others.

Thanks to Miss Owens, I went to the finest schools and finished high school with honors. I went on to college, became a lawyer, and pledged to fight against child abandonment and abuse. I have written a book on neglect and the lack of respect that some people have for each other in this so-called free world.

I am now a motivational speaker, traveling across the nation, in hopes of uplifting those souls that have somehow plummeted downwards into the seas of iniquity.

I share this story about my life today, so that it might prevent others from destroying their tomorrows. I was born from lust and created to tell the truth about its pains. I am not special, but I have bled for the cause of those who felt my sorrow.

Whatever Happened To Forever

*T*his expression, 'Whatever happened to forever?' is often spoken but very seldom understood. It refers to love, and how it will always be a mystery. Forever is a word that speaks about eternity. But we use it to heighten our promises. After all, it works doesn't it? Many of us are victims of bad relationships from one end of the spectrum to the other. This story will hopefully teach you why it's wise to learn to love yourself before you attempt to love someone else.

I am the descendant of love and despair. Since I was a child, I have been taught to forgive the liars and takers of this world. No one truly knows what he or she will be feeling tomorrow. But we all have promised someone that we will still be hopelessly in love with them, if tomorrow should happen to come. If we do not exercise our emotional rights, we shall never become knowledgeable of their strength. For shallow is he who doesn't stop to examine the consequences of such a strong unleashing of emotions. While encountering what we feel is love, we've often found ourselves disengaging from our lifelong expectations.

The subject I am about to speak on is touchy to say the least. But what is life without controversy? I'm not claiming to be an expert, I've just read a lot of nonsense over the years and decided to speak out on this subject myself.

This story will allow you to come along with me as I stroll through the unpredictable male and female minds of this world. I learned first hand that it is many times easier to swim against an ocean's tide than to attempt to dismantle a woman's beliefs.

My name is DeShawn Alexander. I am about six-foot-one with a medium build. My skin is the same color as my mother and father, both native Louisianans. The texture of my hair is soft and curly, like many of the Creoles who live here. My life's work developed through the painful and joyful observations of my family relationships. I studied hard to become a Psychologist.

My father is the kind of man who hopes all the time. He is a man who always says things like, "I hope to win the lottery," or "I hope it doesn't rain." But deep down inside he was hoping Mama would stop the pain. He wasn't born to fail, but many times, my mother would place my father in positions where it was just plain hard to succeed.

I grew up thinking that my father's name was Shawn Alexander, a.k.a. the introverted, perverted son-of-a-so-and-so, at least that's what my mother always called him. He may have been an introvert and maybe even a perverted son-of-a-bitch, but to me he was a good man. Hell, he worked hard and never stayed out late. He was attentive to all my mother's needs. I know a lot of women who would have enjoyed having him around.

My mother's name is Tera Alexander. She wore her hair down past her shoulders, never in any real style. It was just neat and shining and beautiful, like those elite ladies on the cover of stylish hair magazines. At first glance you'd think that she was a modest woman. But she has never seen a reason to humble her tongue. It was a tongue that over the years had become lethal. My mother could win the "Outspoken Words Award" every year. She always felt the need to defend herself, many times before even being blamed. I once overheard her cursing out someone in her sleep.

She has always known that her tongue was sharp. Yet no matter how many examples she's given, she still feels the need to pierce the hearts of others. My mother is a dreamer who has never awakened from her jealous ways. She somehow believed that if she trusted someone, she'd lose her ability to decipher the difference between right and wrong.

I hurt for my mother because she was too confused to hurt for herself. Her anger kept her too weak to fight off her jealous tendencies, which had begun to tarnish her soul. She became so passionate about her envy, until one day it made her passionately lonely. She was taught to distrust anything that resembled a man, and in return she ran off the only man that ever truly loved her.

As a child I was taught (indirectly by my mother) that no matter how hard I tried to be a good man, I would ultimately grow a tail and become a dog just like my father. To my mother, every man had a hidden agenda. She felt that all men had dogmatic traits and it wouldn't be long before I took on my own. .

I have a sister named Tashay, who is two years younger than me. She has one of the purest souls on earth. She always wears a smile and never let's anything upset her. Tashay loves all types of music and has dreamed of becoming a dancer one day. She could see a dance one time and duplicate the steps in a matter of seconds, no matter how difficult the choreography. I have a great relationship with her and we are the best of friends. She graduated from college at the head of her class and now works at a law firm.

She is married to Johnny, who doesn't like to work. He is not a liar that we know of, but he is a genuine taker. The sorry bastard has never even owned a car. She met him on the subway and they were instantly attracted to each other. Sure, he is a nice looking man but damn, a car phobia, please!

Love has sympathetically blinded many of us. So much that every psychiatrist's couch in America is probably occupied as I speak. We all lie there, on the couch, wondering just what brought us to this point. Asking 'Whatever happened to forever?' is a real live look at reality. Somewhere between the first time you say yes and the moment he says, 'I do,' a period of self-imposed amnesia comes over you. How else did such a smart young lady like Tashay end up with such a loser like Johnny?

Early one Saturday morning, like every other Saturday morning, I woke up with sleep in my eyes. I usually get up around nine o'clock, do my chores so that I can get back home to watch college sports on TV. I gathered my clothes and took them over to my mother's house to wash them. I put them into the washing machine and walked down the hallway to say good-morning to my mother. I found her sitting in the living room, a usual place for her.

"Good morning, Mama," I greeted her.

"Good morning, Shawn. What are you doing up so early?"

"I just heard you in here talking back at that TV like you always do." I paused. "Like you expect the people to talk back to you."

"Awe, shut up, Shawn. Come and give your mother a kiss."

My mother recorded TV stories all through the week and watched every last one of them on Saturday with my grandmother. I noticed that my grandmother hadn't come over yet, so I said, "Mama, where is Grandma today?"

"You know Grandma. She's always late. I couldn't wait for her to get here because something good happened on my stories this week. So, she's gonna have to be mad at me for starting without her."

A few minutes later Grandma came walking in. "No, you ain't watching those stories without me," she started in. "You better rewind that shit before I slap you upside your head."

Grandma is a happy-go-lucky soul who keeps everyone laughing. That is, when she isn't stirring up mess. She is nosey as hell, but my guess is, that's what keeps her so energetic about life.

Most of my life's observations for my psychology studies came from our annual family barbecue, always held on July 4th at a local park near our house. It was a time for everyone to get together and catch up on all the family gossip. The most notable family members were my Aunt Jesse and her husband Lester. All the children enjoyed being around them because they were the most entertaining. Though she was a notorious trash-talker, just like Mohammed Ali, she was never afraid to stand up and go toe to toe behind what she felt was right. Another reason we all loved Aunt Jesse was that the adults seemed to hate her for that.

For instance, Aunt Jesse could hear something at 10 o'clock in the morning and by noon our entire family knew about it. She was a 'divulger,' which to us meant that she told things she shouldn't have. Many times she said that it just slipped out. But from what I could tell, Aunt Jesse, like Grandma, just liked stirring up mess. If you needed something advertised, you just ran it across her. Hell, you didn't have to take out any ad. Tell Jesse the news and it would circulate faster than darkness could touch a room at midnight.

Little L and Jennifer are my Uncle Lester's and Aunt Jesse's son and daughter. They are what I call needy. They both sought attention in the worst way. Little L wasn't satisfied unless he was getting the hell beat out of him, and Jennifer was a borderline exhibitionist. While L ran around getting on people's nerves, Jennifer enjoyed showing off her body to whoever would look. Over time, I personally grew to dislike Jennifer because many of my friends knew more about her anatomy than they should have. Her greeting card was her body.

She was even easier to get to know than her father. Hell, by the age of fifty-seven, Uncle Lester had earned the status of a three time All-American-Ho. Aunt Jesse felt that he wasn't worth the raggedy hat he wore on his semi-bald head. But she would say that she stayed with him because she loved the way he gave her special attention.

One memorable night, Uncle Lester and Aunt Jesse were having a typical party at their house. All of the children were in the designated 'children's room' as usual. When one of us cracked the door to peek at the goings on, we all lined up with our heads stacked on top of each other like a totem pole. Watching our parents fascinated us more than anything else. I used to marvel at the way our parents attempted to skate around things they didn't want us to know. Sometimes they'd spell words instead of actually saying them. That was until they figured out that spelling was a class we attended in school, and we were catching on.

Aunt Jesse was a high yellow middle-aged woman with low expectations, and she was a weekend drunk. She didn't mind telling anyone who would listen that she wasn't an alcoholic simply because she didn't go to AA meetings. She kept her family in whatever order she could during the week and went AWOL on the weekends. She was a perplexed individual and I think whatever caused that condition must have trickled into her children's blood as well.

My other uncles said she was built like three days of bad weather. She really didn't have a waist to speak of. Maybe she had even forgotten to stand in the booty line during conception. Most of her hair had fallen out, so she occasionally wore wigs to avoid constant staring.

When her family came over all the cousins knew we were gonna have a nice time. We were gonna have lots of laugh. Ghetto-fide from the cores of their souls to the pits of their nappy hair, this family was, above all, entertaining. My mother said that their ignorance always smelled up the place. However, Tashay and I, and of course, the rest of the cousins, could tolerate the smell of their madness.

My Uncle Joe, my father's oldest brother, is still to this day the funniest man alive. Uncle Joe never ran out of jokes and kept one ready at all times. He is a used car salesman, and by the ladies' standards, a very good looking man. He is about six-foot-three and of average build with salt and pepper hair, which is always well groomed. He never got married and never had any kids.

One day I asked him, "Uncle, why haven't you ever gotten married?"

"Well, I was going to until I met your Aunt Jesse and your Uncle Lester and let's face it, I..." and he paused for a second then said in his lowest voice, " haven't you met their kids? I'm too afraid I'd never be brave enough to attempt a feat like that."

We all laughed at him like we had done so many times over the years.

My father also has a younger brother named Benny. He is a nice looking brother who in my eyes seemed to have it together all the time. He went to college, earned his degree, drove nice cars and dressed impeccably. The female side of the family seemed to have a problem with the fact that he chose not to date black women. Aunt Jesse called him a sellout because he loved white women. To everybody's knowledge, he has never been involved with a black woman. He never misses a family gathering and brings a different white girl along with him every time. I love my Uncle Benny, despite the constant harassment from our narrow-minded family members.

Now what family would be complete without a total mess-up? That is my Uncle Marcus Dewayne, who calls himself M.D. He is a wanna-be rap star, who one day found himself wrapped up in drugs, and seemed to have missed a verse or two in life. He is not a bad looking brother at all. He simply looks at life in a bad way. I don't think he does any real hard drugs, but he hardly remembers the ones that he does use. So I wouldn't call him a functional drug user. To do so, I would have to state his function, and to this day it is unknown.

M.D. has a thing about working. He hates it with a passion. Whenever he comes to a family function, all of the women immediately stop what they're doing. They go and get their purses. They know it won't be long before he starts making a water run and passes a couple of purses on his way. To avoid an issue, they just play it safe.

My mother's brother, Jimmy is as crazy as my Grandma, only louder. On the day he was born, they say Uncle Jimmy came out of the womb running on all fours like a dog. He had wandering eyes and his favorite pastime was looking at women. His wife, my Aunt Jackie, had sent him to the hospital numerous times for getting his eyes stuck on ghetto booty: the same kind that was getting ready to walk by us at that very moment.

As is typical at our reunions, mothers and fathers had gone their separate ways to begin their annual male and female bonding. We cousins were all getting along, but before you knew it three ghetto-queens started walking towards us. I could feel the tension in the air and knew that it wouldn't be long before some trouble started jumping off.

I turned to Tashay and said, "Do you see what I see?"

"Yes, I sure do. I'm gonna get a little closer so I can watch Aunt Jackie beat Uncle Jimmy down again."

Like clock work, as soon as Uncle Jimmy looked over, Aunt Jackie threw one of her sandals and knocked him in the back of that big head of his.

"Jimmy! Haven't I done told you about disrespecting me? You old drunk, disrespectful fool! You better turn around and eat the rest of that chicken on your plate and act like your ass is married, you old-bubble-eyed-fool."

She continued her ranting. "You look just like a fish, right before feeding time, every time a piece of tail passes by, your mouth pops wide open. You can't handle what you've got at home. You, no-stamina-having-bastard!" When she said that everyone started laughing, and it never seem to bother Uncle Jimmy one bit. By then he was quite used to all of her antics.

The three ghetto-queens just kept on walking towards us. That's when Uncle Junior, my mother's youngest brother, started to yell at them like a dog in heat.

"Hey, now look at all that jelly. Man, I feel like a loaf of bread. Excuse me ladies, could I interest any one of you in a loaf of bread?"

My mother stood, rising off the park bench, and threw up one of her hands. "You nasty little dog," she said. "I have told you about carrying on like that around my husband. Junior, I don't play that, you know that I'll cut you, now don't you? You better get control of your third leg before I thump you in one of those little balls of yours."

The girls were getting ready to stop and talk to him, when my mother hollered out, "Jackie girl, I see some creep-crawlers that need to be sprayed!" All of a sudden my mother and Aunt Jackie started spraying insect repellent in their direction.

The ghetto-queens saw them coming towards them. I guess they felt outnumbered and knew that it wasn't time to prove how brave they were. They changed direction and just kept on walking.

"Shawn, what's wrong with your crazy wife?" Uncle Junior asked.

"Junior, she was your sister before she was my wife. You know how she is. You know she's got a short fuse and a sharp tongue, so why did you take her there?"

My mother was a mild drinker. She was already a handful to deal with sober. Everyone knew that when she was intoxicated, she was not the one to be messing with. But my Uncle Junior didn't care, and so they went at it.

"Junior, just because you are a dog, doesn't mean that you've got a right to shake your fleas on everybody else."

"Girl, why are you tripping? Being a dog ain't contagious."

"Yeah, but it's those fleas that are harder to get rid of than they are to get. So don't stand so close to my husband while you're trying to catch them okay?"

During my sophomore year in high school, my father moved out of the house, but I never really understood why until years later. I didn't know it at the time but some of those same fleas had already bit my mother. It turned out that my mother had just as much dog in her as Uncle Junior had in him. I found out what happened from the horse's mouth, the best place to gather the truth. What was revealed still haunts me to this day

By that time I was attending a local junior college. One particular day between classes I decided to go over and visit my mother. When I got there I used my key to let myself in. I walked in on her looking through some old photos.

"Mama, what are you doing?"

"What does it look like I'm doing?"

There was a long silence, until finally she said with a low tone, "I'm just sorting out some pictures and reminiscing, that's all." She sat there holding a picture of my father in her hand.

"Mama, what are you doing to yourself?"

She shuffled the pictures quickly, hoping that I didn't catch her. She said, "Child, what do you think I'm doing to myself?"

"Come on, Mama. Now you know that I caught you looking at those pictures of Daddy." I looked straight at her and asked, "Are you ever gonna tell me what really happened to you and him?"

"We just couldn't make it, that's all."

"Mama, that worked on me years ago. I'm old enough to deal with the truth, so cut the shit."

"You better watch your mouth boy!"

"Mama, don't try to get off the subject. I'm ready to hear the truth!" I demanded.

"Okay, then set yourself down."

I sat down in a small chair near the window in the living room and prepared myself for a version of a story I had longed to hear for years.

"Well, Shawn. My life has been all one big lie. I used to tell you that your father was unfaithful. Well, I lied. I was the unfaithful one."

A part of me wanted her to stop as soon as I heard that confession, but I knew this was hard for her to say, so I wasn't about to interrupt her. Tears began to run down her beautiful face as she gave her account of the truth. Who would have thought a bright family atmosphere held such dark secrets? It was difficult to believe my mother was guilty of such unwarranted, immoral acts.

"One day, I was hanging out with some of my old high school classmates at the mall. We were just window-shopping and talking shit to each other like we always did. We ran into an old friend of ours named Kenny Morrison that day..."

I interrupted, "You mean, the good looking, athletic, but drugged out Kenny Morrison?"

"Yes, that's right. You've heard of him?"

"Yes, my dad couldn't stand him. Mama, you didn't, did you?"

"I don't want to talk about it anymore."

"Oh, yeah. We are gonna talk, and talk right now." I looked straight at her and continued, "I can't believe that all this time you've lead us to believe that Dad was no good. How could you have done something like that?"

"Your father was always away on business."

"Yes, trying to support his family while you were around here supporting your habits," I shot back.

"It wasn't like that at all!" Her sad voice rang in my ears.

I knew that it was hurting her to tell me the truth. My going off that way was only making matters worse, so I got up and walked into the kitchen. I leaned on the counter and attempted to rationalize the information she had just given me.

She got up and followed me. "So you think that this has been easy for me? I have lived with this for years..."

I cut her short, "Mama, are you listening to yourself? Can you hear what you're saying? All I'm hearing is, 'I this, and I that.' When you gave birth to me and Tashay, you were no longer only 'I.' What about 'us,' Mama? What you did was selfish and there is nothing you can say to undo what has already been done. How long did this go on, Mama?" She turned her back on me. "When did my dad find out?" I persisted.

In her lowest voice she finally replied, "About a year and a half later, I guess."

"Mama, this went on for almost two years?" I asked. I was incredulous.

She didn't answer that question. Instead she placed her chin on her chest. I was no doubt causing her a great deal of embarrassment. After a few seconds had passed she looked up and said, "One day Kenny and I got careless and had sex without protection. I came up pregnant."

"Did he find out that you had an abortion?"

"I never had an abortion."

"What in the hell are you saying, Mama?"

"Baby, Tashay is not your father's child."

"Tashay is Kenny's daughter," I stated, completely devoid of emotion.

There I was, standing in front of the woman who had given birth to me. I felt so betrayed. I didn't know who to hurt for the most, my sister, my dad or myself. There was one thing for sure; my mother wasn't part of that consideration.

"After your father and I had you, we decided to have no more children. He went to the doctor and got fixed. It was normal for me to miss a period every now and then. I thought nothing of it until it was too late. Your father knew from the beginning though. Haven't you ever heard that this world is smaller than we know? Well, one of your father's co-workers lived in the same building as Kenny and my friend, Sandy. He saw a picture of me on your father's desk one day and said, 'Shawn, man, who is this?' 'Do you know her?' he replied.

"Not knowing that the girl in the picture was me, he said, 'I see this person all the time over at my apartment complex.'

"'This girl?' your father asked reluctantly.

"'Yes, that same girl in that picture.'

"'There can't be two women who look that much alike,' he said.

"'She comes over to see a brother name Kenny, an ex-football player. You know, the one who got hooked on drugs and lost everything. I think his last name is Morrison, or something like that. Well anyway, at least two or three times a week she's over there. She never really stays late, just long enough to have sex and then she leaves,' he told your dad."

"Mama, how did you get all of this information?"

"Your father and I talked about it from time to time."

"That had to have been tough on him," I sighed. "Okay, go on," I encouraged her.

"The man told your father that I never stayed long and that he heard us carrying on upstairs. After he told your Dad what he knew, he asked him, 'So, how do you know her, Shawn?'

"Your father told me that he turned to him and said, 'Andrew,' that was the man's name, 'she was my wife at one time.'

"We were still married but he couldn't dare tell the man. He had so much pride. It took him forever to confront me."

"What?"

"Yes, he held onto the secret until I was in my fourth month of pregnancy when I was beginning to show. I guess he felt avoiding the confrontation would make it all go away. Though I had humiliated him he still loved me more than anything in this whole world. While laying in the bed one night I was awakened by these words, 'Tera, do you have something you want to tell me?' I held my breath for what felt like hours. The lights were out and I could see the side of his face from what little light was seeping in from outside. He was a proud man and tried not to lose his composure. As I turned to answer him, I could see tears streaming down the side of his face.

"After a long pause, I finally said, 'I don't really know where to start, Shawn.'

"'Well, whenever you start, please, do me one last favor. Let whatever you end up saying be the truth.'

"Before I could start speaking, he said, 'How far along are you?' There I was laying in bed with my husband getting ready to admit to him, that not only was I having an affair but that I was four and a half months pregnant by another man.

"'I am four months pregnant,' I told him.

"'Tera, that is not my only question, but I do feel that it's a fair question to ask, don't you?'

"'Sure, Baby,' I said.

"'Please don't call me Baby while you're carrying another man's child. I feel you at least owe me that decency.'

"'Yes, I do,' I said. 'I have no other choice but to have it. I'm too far along to have an abortion.'

"'Tera, haven't I tried to be a good husband to you?' he asked me. 'I've never wanted a five bedroom house. BMW's are not my favorite cars, but I saw to it that you drove the one you wanted, didn't I?'

"'Sure you did,' was all I could say.

"'Now, I admit I haven't been able to give you a lot of my time, but it has taken all the time I have available to acquire these nice things for you.'

"Your father reached out to me and held me in his arms as we both cried ourselves to sleep."

"Whatever happened to Kenny Morrison?" I asked.

"When he found out I was pregnant, he ran faster than he did playing football."

"Well?"

"Well, what?"

"What happened next?"

"About six weeks later, I went to meet Kenny over at his apartment. My so-called best friend Sandy, who just happened to be his cousin, was sharing a place with him at the time. When I got there the door was cracked so I let myself in."

"What happened then?"

"I saw another woman coming out of Kenny's bedroom, just laughing and carrying on. She said, 'Oh, come right on in, you must be Sandy's friend?' She called out, 'Sandy, someone's here for you.' Not knowing who I was she introduced herself as Kenny's girlfriend. She said that he just stepped out for a minute to get some ice so that they could make some drinks. She asked, 'Would you like to stay and have a drink with us?'"

After a deep breath my mother continued, "By that time, Sandy came out of her room wearing her dazzling smile that she lost faster than the time it took for Mike Tyson to knock out Michael Spinks. I stared at her and asked, 'Sandy, girl, what's going on?

"'Tera, let's go outside and let me talk to you.'

"I looked at her with tears sweltering in my eyes and said, 'No, that's all right Sandy. It's raining outside, and besides I'm pregnant.' She hadn't known.

"'Tera, girl I'm sorry, is there anything that I can do?'

"'No, from the looks of everything, it seems like you've done enough,' was all I could say.

"'Girl, I tried to tell you that he wasn't worth all your troubles but you just had to have him. You knew that when Kenny started back drinking he would eventually start back using. Girl, he ain't worth it. Kenny is a smooth-talking cokehead with two bad habits: women and drugs. I told you that, but you wouldn't listen, Tera. Now you're gonna blame me for all of this?'

"It wasn't but a couple of seconds later when Kenny came walking in, smiling like he had just signed an N.F.L. contract. I asked, 'And why are you so happy today Kenny?'

"He hadn't seen me yet, but when he heard my voice, he dropped his smile like a bad habit. By the time our eyes met, his girlfriend had come out of the room. She was walking towards him wearing the robe I had bought him two weeks prior to this whole mess.

"So I said, 'Kenny, tell whatever her name is to disrobe herself.'

"The girlfriend responded, 'What is she, Kenny, some kind of freak? You know that I don't get down like that. I'm into men, sweetie, and men only.'

"'Well, right now you're in a robe that I bought Kenny, and I don't appreciate you wearing it. So take it off now or else!'

"'Or else what?' she asked.

"She turned to Kenny and demanded, 'Kenny are you just going to stand there and let her talk to me like this?'

"I couldn't take it anymore. I was too far gone to get an abortion, too married to lie, and by that time, too proud to cry. Before I knew it, I was grabbing at the robe. Everyone was disrespecting me and I needed to feel better about what was happening. After all, she was trying to clown me. Sandy knew that I didn't play, so she just got her scary self out of the way. Within a matter a minutes, I had torn the robe off of her and left her lying there in a fetal position. She was holding the back of her head with both hands, hoping that the worst was over."

My mother continued recounting the event. "As I rose up off of her I said, 'Don't ever disrespect me again, especially while you're wearing something that I bought. Do you hear me? Do you hear me?'

"I looked down at her and said, 'You better protect yourself and brush your teeth real good for the next couple of weeks, so that you can get the rest of my taste out of your mouth.'"

"Mama, you didn't say that."

"Yes, I did, Shawn. I was mad as hell, and on top of all that I was hurting bad. When I got home your father was there, just waiting on me, being his usual calm self.

"'Tera, are you tired yet?' he asked. 'What else can you do to humiliate me?' How much more mud are you willing to drag my feelings through? I just got a call from my friend who lives in the same apartment complex as Sandy. He told me that you were over to her house earlier today. I love you, Tera, more than you'll ever know, and

I'm willing to remain by your side. That is if you won't ask me to relinquish any more of my pride.'"

"So what did you say to that?" I asked her.

"I got down on my knees and kissed your father's feet. I promised him that I would never do it again. Five months later Tashay was born and your dad treated her as if she was his very own. So much so that even you, to this day, thought that she was his. Your father was a hell of a man, but when you were about sixteen years old he went out of town on business and I betrayed him once again.

"Kenny had come back into town and told Sandy that he wanted to see Tashay. Reluctantly I took her over to see him. On the way Tashay had fallen asleep in the car. When I went upstairs to the apartment, Kenny seemed very nervous about meeting her, so I didn't press the issue."

"So, Mama, what happened?"

"I did something very stupid."

"Mama. Please."

"I fell prey to his charm once again. When I gave myself to him then, I lost your dad for good."

After hearing my mother's story, I felt very deceived, but I had greater respect for my father. My father worked long and hard for years to allow my mother to finish college. He never told me his side of the story. He had to have been hurting knowing some other man had been sleeping with his wife, but he never wanted us to lose respect for our mother.

I have attended many weddings since hearing my mother's side of the story, and have often heard couples repeat their vows in almost every way imaginable. 'Forever' is usually the critical word. My mother probably did love my father in some way, but 'forever' wasn't one of them. She loved her selfish fantasies more than the realities of her family's world.

About five or six years later I received my degree in Psychology. I became a practitioner and opened my own office on the other side of town. I focused on relationships. I guess you could say that I had become fascinated with the law of love. The thought of love, or the lack of love, had me spellbound to a point of no return. I'd known for some time that love knows no one person, and it has no set destination.

I studied the pros and cons of relationships for years, and spent endless hours attempting to analyze the heart. I have learned so much, yet no matter how much information we gather in this area, we will still be unable to gauge the human hearts. The moral aspects of a person can form too many branches, and like a tree's are intertwined and far-reaching. Although so many of us feel that we are strong, the painful truth is at times we are emotionally inadequately prepared to take on the beast of love.

Though the deception of love's emotion fascinates me, it is the use of words that help to formulate the sensations necessary to create the submissive desires of man. Words can be used to invoke the animal instincts so many of us deny we possess. The unveiling of these emotions often leaves us helpless and many times ashamed. So many of us simply wish to preclude any notions of having these characteristics.

My mother loved my father with her words, and lost him with her actions. She allowed a smooth conversation to soften her senses. She became putty in the hands of a fool. Her inability to remain strong caused her to give in to a foolish weakness. She gave away her love, love that years ago she had sworn to give only to my father. Fornication is not a crime, but can become a complex sin, as demonstrated by my mother. It does not automatically send your soul to hell but it does start the process.

Many of my clients are victims of emotional assault. I've learned that pain has no identifiable characteristic, that a smile is only as genuine as its owner. Though I am intrigued by the promise of emotional stability, I'm often discouraged by the lack of effort used to prevent many of these emotional reoccurrences. The very second I feel like I have this whole thing figured out, something always happens to nullify my findings. There is one thing for sure, love has never known 'forever.'

One day while reviewing some files at my desk, my secretary, Claudia, buzzed to say I had a visitor.

"Who is it?" I asked.

"It's your Aunt Jesse."

"Tell her to come right in."

As Aunt Jesse came walking through the door, I could tell she was in a different mood. She wasn't wearing that vivacious smile I had grown accustomed to seeing. Before I could get up out of my chair to greet her, she began to cry.

"Aunt Jesse, what's wrong?" I asked with great concern.

She just stood there with a look of shame upon her face. She shook her head back and forth in frustration. I was reaching deep into my emotional grab bag as I stretched my hands towards her. My aunt had fallen prey to life's frightening fanfare. This person, who as children we regarded as being forever strong, had obviously become momentarily weak. The look in her eyes allowed me to see through to the pain inside her heart. She came to me in her most important hour, hoping I could ease her discomfort. It is my belief that we are not unlike airplanes. No matter what our destination is in life, nor how high we fly, there will come a time when we are in dire need of an emotional refueling.

As I reached deeper into my bag, I knew whatever I took out must be the answer my Aunt Jesse searched for. She is allergic to wool and I knew that I wouldn't be given the chance to pull any over her eyes. She was a lot of things, but stupid wasn't one of them. As soon as I saw the tears, I proceeded to move in with caution. Asking her questions that, if answered truthfully, would ultimately lead her to answer her own questions.

Even though she was hurting, she was attempting to hold on to what little pride she had left. Many times in life it is that same pride that imprisons us and immobilizes our dreams. As I looked into her eyes, I could feel the same hurt inside my father's heart. I was taught not to allow my personal thoughts to enter the room, but I couldn't help it. Hell, off the record, I was just keeping it real.

When Aunt Jesse spoke, she said, "Child, I was told you are one of those men who listens to problems, and do I have my share of them. First of all, I need to tell you that I am on a fixed income and I don't have much money, but I can take you out to lunch. You don't have to lay me down on that expensive couch over there."

She might have had a lot of pain inside her heart, but through it all she was still entertaining.

"Aunt Jesse, what's wrong? Have a seat and tell me all about it."

"Baby, how much is it gonna cost me to sit in that little chair over there against the wall?"

"Aunt Jesse, it's not going to cost you anything at all to sit down and talk to me."

"We can walk and talk for all I care, I just need someone to talk to that's all."

"Does this have anything to do with Uncle Lester?

"I guess you've heard that I haven't been feeling well lately?"

"No, I haven't heard anything about your health."

"I've been married to your Uncle Lester for over thirty years now, and, if you can believe it, that old bugger left me for a younger woman."

"Oh, Aunt Jesse. I'm so sorry to hear that."

"You're not as sorry as he is!"

"Are you sure that he's with another woman Aunt Jesse?"

"Am I sure? Lil-Shawn, I may be getting old, but I am not blind. Hell yeah, I'm sure! I even caught them together a few weeks ago. They were standing on the corner of 15th and McCarthy." She paused and dabbed away the tears from the corners of her eyes. "Yes, it was him, and they were hugged up next to his old Cadillac like two balls in a nut sack."

I couldn't keep from laughing at her. Through her pain, I was delighted her hilarious, yet racy commentary was still alive.

"Did he see you, Aunt Jesse?"

"Hell no, his eyes were all in that heifer's ear. His nose was so wide open, you could have parked a couple of cars in it."

"Well, did you say anything to them?"

"They were far away for me to shoot them. There were too many cars in front of me to speed up and run them over. Plus I had a friend in the car with me. I didn't want her to see them, so I played it off and acted like nothing was wrong. I just went and dropped my friend off at her house as planned, and waited on Lester to bring his old tail home."

"So when he came home what did you do?"

"I did what any other woman would have done if they had seen their husband hugged up with another woman. I stood behind the front door and when he came walking in, I busted him over the head with a frying pan."

"No, you didn't do that Aunt Jesse. Did you hurt him?"

"Hurt him? Hell. How long have you known me, Child? Your Uncle Lester had been working real hard for that ass-whupping and when he came in the house, it was time for him to get paid."

"What was his response?"

"Baby, have you ever been hit over the head with a cast-iron skillet? If you get hit hard enough, you can't say anything until you wake up."

"Damn, Aunt Jesse. You didn't knock him out, did you?"

"You better know it. He was walking around for about a week with a knot on his head as big as an A-cup."

My Aunt Jesse was something else. She said all of that with a straight face. It was all I could do to fight off the laughter.

"What did the young lady look like?" I asked.

"You know, she was a pretty typical looking tramp. You know the type, all butt and no brains. The type that is always searching for a sugar daddy. I told Lester that he should tell her the truth."

"And what is the truth, Aunt Jesse?" I asked.

"Your Uncle Lester needs to tell her that he ain't no sugar daddy! If anything he's Sweet-and-Low. But, Child, Lester ain't been sweet since he fell into the chocolate when he was a child on Halloween. Even then he was only sweet because he was full of candy."

"What else did you say to him?"

"That he needed to keep his little tramp indoors, before her ugly head explodes one day."

"Aunt Jesse, what do you mean by that?"

"You know. She was already an airhead, so you tell me what was going to happen if she gets a few more good whiffs of air? Her pumped up head might explode!"

That was it, when she said that I lost all of my professionalism. I fell on the floor laughing. I couldn't control myself any longer. Aunt Jesse had convinced me that she was no fool, and I was having the time of my life. As I listened to her, she continued to pour her heart out to me in the most hilarious way.

"Child," she went on, "I told him a long time ago if he wanted a great big butt, he should have stayed his funny looking self in the country and married a cow."

"Okay, okay, let me get hold of myself," I said. "What's next Aunt Jesse? Where do we go from here? Do you feel that there's any hope for your marriage?"

"I guess that is really hard to say right now. I mean I still love him and all, but..."

"But what?"

"I can't stand seeing them together, and every time I do, I want to hurt him for hurting me. You see Lil-Shawn, I believed in your uncle when no one else did. Now, he has forgotten about me."

"Have you ever stopped to think that maybe you played a part in all of this?" I knew the direct questioning would hurt. "Maybe there was something you did that has him running into someone else's arms? Now before you answer that question, take a few deep breaths and try, if you can, to remove the anger from the equation. Answer my question from that space inside your heart where you store the truth."

She sat there with a look of embarrassment upon her face. She knew where this had all started and that now she was dealing with reality. More than three minutes went by before Aunt Jesse pulled her chin off of her chest. She seemed ready to deal with the truth that had been haunting her for years. At the height of her emotional demise, she had come to me, her nephew, and I was about to be her confidant. I gathered more inside information than I had bargained for.

Attempting to console another human being's emotions in hopes of unveiling their troubles can be a heart-wrenching experience to say the least. Aunt Jesse had finally opened up her emotional doors and gave me permission to enter her world. Here sat a woman, who, at one time in her life, I felt was too tough to be moved by anything. But she proved to be human and as vulnerable as a newborn baby.

"I gave him the best years of my life," she said. "I suffered along side a man who had found it easier to give up rather than to place his feet firmly back on the ground and fight."

"Aunt Jesse, if you don't mind me asking, what does giving your all really mean to you?"

She placed her chin back on her chest and there was a moment of silence. When she spoke she said, "My all. My all is all that I have to give."

"Are you sure that you've given Uncle Lester absolutely everything you have to give?" I pressed. "Have you asked him what it was that caused him to stray? Have you ever asked him what he really needed from you as his wife?"

"No, but why should I have to ask him? He's the man in this marriage. He should be telling me what he wants without being asked."

"Are you sure that he's never told you what he wanted? Will you believe me if I were to tell you that not all men have the ability to express themselves, just as not all women have the ability to listen?"

"I guess that's true, because I sometimes hear only what I want to hear," she acknowledged. "Lester has told me many times what he wants me to do, but I haven't been able to submit to it in all these years."

"What is that?"

"As far back as I can remember, he has been asking me to leave the lights on while we were having sex, but I refuse to."

"What are you saying, Aunt Jesse?"

"Baby, your Uncle Lester has never seen me fully undressed since we've been together."

"Aunt Jesse," I breathed. I was practically speechless. "That's a long time not to have shown yourself to the person you love."

"I know. I've just never been comfortable enough with my body to show it to him in that way."

"What happens when two are having sex?"

"Well, most of the time when I come out of the bathroom, I have my robe on. Your Uncle Lester lays on his side with his back turned to me, in an attempt to respect my wishes."

"Wait one minute. Do you mean to tell me that he has never made love to you with the lights on?"

"Yes, that's exactly what I'm saying. Never."

"Well, I guess by now Uncle Lester must be pretty good at seeing things in the dark?"

"You've got that right."

"Where did this all start, Aunt Jesse?"

She knew where to look. "Well, I guess it all started when I was about eleven years old. My parents were going out one night, so I had a babysitter named Tonya, who was about seventeen at the time. After taking my bath I went down in the basement to watch TV with Tonya. We were just sitting there, laughing and carrying on. It was an old Richard Pryor comedy tape that my father watched over and over again, and Tonya and I watched it together that night."

I was wondering where she was going with this but didn't dare interrupt her. I just listened quietly as Aunt Jesse recounted her story.

"We were sitting next to each other when Richard Pryor started talking about oral sex. I really didn't know what it was all about, but it wasn't long before I found out. Tonya turned around and asked me if I knew what oral sex was.

"I replied, 'Sure I guess so, but that's nasty.'

"Then she said, 'No, only at certain times of the month.'

"She got up and turned on the light. She took her panties off and stood in front of me, playing with herself and looking straight into my eyes."

"What did you do then?"

"Well I just sat there and watched her for a while. And then she told me to take my panties off and try it myself, so I did. I didn't see anything wrong with it, I mean it was my body and no one was around to tell me not to. I was trying to do it like she was but I wasn't getting the same reaction at all. So I stopped.

"'What's wrong, don't you like playing with yourself?' she asked.

"'No, not really, it's a silly thing to do,' I replied.

"I started to put my panties back on but she got down on her knees and touched my private area with her finger. I knew that what she was doing was wrong, but before I knew what was happening, I was on my back and she was still touching me.

"I felt ashamed, yet my body was on fire. I never saw Tonya again after that night. Even though many years have passed I still feel the shame as strongly today as I felt it that night. I haven't spoken about it until now though."

"Why haven't you told Uncle Lester or anyone else for that matter?"

"Because I feel no one will understand how an eleven year old girl could allow that to happen to her. Besides, I have always felt people would think I'm gay. There are times when I have a desire to make love to your Uncle Lester with the lights on, but a sense of shame always seems to come over me.

"Your Uncle Lester has threatened to leave me over it on many occasions but I held my ground and never gave in. Up until now, he was just an old man with wandering eyes. Now he's an even older man with wandering hands, trying to touch everything within reach."

"Aunt Jesse, for years I have listened to the broken hearts of this world and heard their unspoken truths. I have seen clear images of things that, still to this day, most people have not been able to focus on."

"What does all of that mean, Lil-Shawn?"

"It simply means that often times we're just a block or two away from peace, yet we choose to walk next door to deception."

"Are you telling me to hang in there and wait around on my husband until he gets finished messing with this bimbo?"

"It is easier to grasp the thought of mixing oil with water than to comprehend mending the heart of a woman who has been scorned," I replied.

"All that sounds great but what am I supposed to do with myself while he treats me this way?"

"Stand where he can see you clearly and go on with your life. Fix him dinner and keep yourself clean. Wash his clothes as well as his floors, and last but not least, never forget to say goodnight. It was because of your anger he sought out other women and it will be because of your love he returns. I'm not telling you to cater to his madness, nor to accept him being with another woman. Just listen to the things he has not yet learned to express.

"Never allow anyone to get you angry enough to inflict bodily harm again. Aunt Jesse. I watched you over the years say some very mean things to Uncle Lester, and I've never seen him retaliate verbally or physically. Some things invoke certain reactions and even though dating someone else is a bit extreme, we don't have to revert to pointing fingers and hitting people over the head with frying pans. I know that you're not ready to leave, because if you were, you would not be here. Sometimes we are the cause of our own pain and we are almost never ready to admit it.

"If you want to be sure, then do your part. When you've done all you know how to do and you can no longer be with him, I'll come by and pick you up. We'll go down and begin the divorce proceedings.

"Many of us are unable to receive these last couple of statements. So brace yourself for the hard facts. You see, our pride alone will not allow us to decompose our own actions. It is human nature to blame others for our shortcomings. Believe me when I say that it is healthier to succumb to the truth, than to surrender to the suffocating facts that our hearts aren't willing to unfold. Haven't you heard that if we invite a lie into our hearts, we will undoubtedly take it into our homes? Stop hitting him over the head with your hands and stroke his heart with love," I advised.

"Now, I need you to come back here at the same time next week and give me an update. If you can, try to bring Uncle Lester with you. Tell him I want to have a talk with you two together." Aunt Jesse got up and gave me a hug as we said our good-byes.

I had listened to several clients that day, but the time I spent with Aunt Jesse remained heavy on my heart. I felt too young to have dedicated myself to dissecting the dismembered emotions of mankind. Though these sessions would many times take their toll on me, I continued to press forward in my quest for the vindicating messages necessary to help uplift my people.

I mastered the notion that it was easier but not better to stand in judgment of a man than it is to stand in his shoes. It is also better to inquire than to wonder, just as it is better to listen than to speak. I knew that it would take Aunt Jesse and Uncle Lester all the time they had left to live on this earth to figure out what had gone wrong, yet I was giving them only a week to assemble their defenses.

We are a world full of defenders, and no matter what our actions entail, if given enough time to ponder our wrongs, it seems inevitable that we will find something right about the wrong we've done.

A week went by and Uncle Lester and Aunt Jesse came to my office.

"Hello, Lil-Shawn. I haven't seen you in a while, son," Uncle Lester said.

"Yes, I know, it's been some time."

"Uncle Lester, where is Aunt Jesse?"

He turned to look as he responded, "She was right behind me when I was walking down the hall. I don't know where she is." He smiled and took advantage of our moment alone. "Well, I guess she came in here and told you that I had a young-tender in my life."

"Now, Uncle Lester, I'm a psychologist and I can't tell you what Aunt Jesse and I discuss unless she gives me permission to tell you."

Just as I said that, Aunt Jesse walked in and sat down. "I was about to come looking for you," I said.

"Hell, I'm not the one who's lost. It's him," she responded and nodded towards her husband.

"Please, let's not start taking shots at each other," I pleaded.

"I thought we came in here to work things out," she stated.

"Oh, is that what this is all about?" asked Uncle Lester. "I knew things were a little fishy when she asked me to come with her. She didn't have to lie to get me to come see you. You're my nephew and that alone is a good enough reason to come and visit. But anyway, we're here. Are you going to try and help us work things out?"

"Yes, that is my objective," I replied.

"I don't mind talking, I just want to be heard," he said.

"If his damn ass knew how to talk, I'd be happy to listen to his stupid ass," Aunt Jesse piped in.

"You see, Lil-Shawn, that's what I've had to live with for over thirty years now and I'm tired of her speaking to me like that."

"OK you two, now here is how it's going to go," I interjected. "I'm going to let Uncle Lester speak first. After he's finished I will allow you to speak, Aunt Jesse. Before you start though, let me tell you first that there is hope for the two of you. Aunt Jesse came in here to see me last week with a heavy heart, and today, despite all of your problems, you two have agreed to come in here together.

"So let's start off by saying that we all want to be here. Can we at least say that?" I looked at both of them while they nodded.

"Sure," said Uncle Lester."

"I guess that's true," agreed Aunt Jesse.

"Okay, then. Let's begin. Uncle Lester, do you still love your wife?"

He didn't answer right away. He just sat there with a blank expression on his face. "Okay then let me rephrase the question, since you're having a problem answering me."

"No," said Uncle Lester. "No, I mean, no you don't have to rephrase the question. I do still love my wife. I've just gotten tired of being talked down to. So I've found someone who would listen to me and not put me down all the time."

"Why do you feel that she's putting you down?"

"You're asking me that like I don't understand English. I know that she puts me down and I'm not going to spend another thirty years of my life biting my tongue!"

"When is the last time you told her you loved her?"

"To tell you the truth, I really don't know. It's been some time ago."

"Well, did you stop loving her some time ago, and that's why you haven't told her?"

"No, I stopped feeling loved."

I knew that we were close to a breakthrough and when I asked my next question, everything came to the surface.

"Uncle Lester, honestly, how long do you think that a relationship like you're having now can last? Before you answer, I want you to think back on the hard times that you two have gone through. Try to picture yourself going through those hard times tomorrow, without Aunt Jesse."

They both grew quiet as an aura of calmness lingered in the room. Finally, Uncle Lester said, "Lil-Shawn, I'm not getting any younger. I don't want to run the streets anymore. I just want your Aunt Jesse to stop treating me like a child, that's all."

"Well, Aunt Jesse, what are you thinking at this very moment?"

She turned to him. "Why didn't you tell me this instead of making me look like a fool?" she asked.

"Can you hear yourself? It's always been about you," said Uncle Lester. "I know I'm not the greatest looking man in this world, but do you have to remind me about it everyday? I'm tired of being called ugly. It hurts to be called that by everyone in the streets, and then to come home and hear it from your own wife is even worse.

"You're not the best built person in the world yourself, but I'm not always putting that in your face, am I? I don't want another woman in my life, but if you're not going to respect me as a man, then I'm going to leave you."

They were finally dealing with their issues and all I had to do was moderate from that point on. They were sitting on opposite ends of the couch at first, but by the end of the session, they were holding hands and kissing.

"Oh, Lester, I'm sorry for not respecting you. Can you ever forgive me?"

"Sure, I can. I love you," he replied.

"I'm going to work on my anger and from this moment on, if I don't have anything good to say, then I won't say anything at all," said Aunt Jesse.

"Man, if all of my sessions went like this I could take a couple of days off and play golf."

My uncle began to cry tears of joy. They continued to hold hands and looked into each other's eyes. Just watching them reconnecting was choking me up.

"So, where do we go from here?" Uncle Lester asked Aunt Jesse.

"Honey tonight our bedroom is going to remind you of a Motel 6," said Aunt Jesse.

"What in the hell does that mean?" asked Uncle Lester.

She just smiled at him and whispered, "Well, Baby, when you come to bed tonight, I'm going to leave the light on for you."

My Uncle Lester's eyes opened up wider than a drawbridge as he smiled from ear to ear. He gave me a hug and left to go outside for a smoke before Aunt Jesse came out to the car.

Aunt Jesse stayed a moment to say, "I almost forgot to tell you. Your cousin, Jennifer, is having a birthday party over at her house this weekend and she wanted me to tell you you're invited."

"Okay, tell her I'll be there and not to worry."

"I've have got to go now. Look, Baby, I have to go by The Home Depot. I have to get some of those 100-watt bulbs, so my Lester can see everything. You take care."

I smiled at her and felt an enormous sense of satisfaction.

I made it to my cousin Jennifer's birthday party that weekend. It was a lot of things, but boring was not one of them. As a child, I didn't really like hanging around my cousin because of the lack of clothes she wore. As a young girl, Jennifer was about as easy to catch as a drop of rain in a thunderstorm. I knew that if all else failed, I could leave her party and go to a nearby club that was always jumping. When I got to Jennifer's house, I could tell that it was going to be a long night.

Jennifer remained true to form and was wearing something resembling a dinner napkin and some pumps when she greeted me at the front door. She had never paid me much attention, and her friendliness scared me. "Hey, Lil-Shawn, what's going on?" she said.

I couldn't believe it when she took my coat. She turned to me and said, "Long time no see cuz. I've really missed you, how long has it been, this time?"

I couldn't stop looking at her attire, or should I say the lack thereof. I was so busy staring at her; I didn't hear anything she had just said. She had to repeat, "Shawn, how long has it been, this time?"

"Oh, several years I'm sure," I managed to reply. Her large rear hanging out of her 'skirt' prompted me to say,

"Jennifer, my cousin, I see that you haven't changed one bit."

"Was I supposed to? Now Shawn, you know that I've never been shy."

"Yes, how could anyone ever forget?"

"I wouldn't let anyone forget that, now would I?" She took my hand and said, "Come go with me, I'd like to introduce you to some friends of mine."

As I met her friends, the phrase 'birds of a feather…' came to mind. There I was, surrounded by more half-naked women than the swimsuit portion of a beauty pageant. If I had wanted to do a study on the black anatomy, I had come to the right place.

"Hey girl, this is my cousin, Shawn. You know, the cousin, I'm always telling you all about?"

"You were right girl, he sure is fine," her friend said.

"Shawn, this is Renee. Renee, this is Shawn. I told you, Nay Nay, my cousin was fine. Why don't you two just get to know each other while I make sure that everyone's okay."

She walked away smiling like she was the newest dating game host. Sure. Renee was kind of cute, but she looked to be as used up as a ten-year-old rent-a-car. It didn't take me long to know that I was out of my element. I felt like a soon to be claimed twenty-dollar bill floating around inside a crack house. But I decided to let the conversation begin

I was hit by the big three 'No- No's' of dating questions right off the bat: 'where do you work?' 'how much money do you make a year?' and 'what kind of car do you drive?'

I knew how to answer those questions in a way that would probably hurt Renee's feelings, but I simple asked, 'Before taxes or after?'

I knew she wasn't expecting such a smart-ass reply and she made a quick exit. "Well I see a friend over there that I haven't seen in a while, it was really nice meeting you," she said as she disappeared into the crowd.

Just as I was getting ready to pour myself a drink, Jennifer reappeared with another one of her under-dressed friends. I thought to myself, damn, now what do you know, a 'ho' upgrade. Her name was Tish and she was gorgeous. But it didn't take me three minutes to find out that gorgeous was all she was. I know I was a little selective, but just like on the daytime soap opera, I only have 'One Life to Live.'

I decided to make the best of it and at least give her a try. So I said, "Hello, Tish, what are you drinking tonight?"

"I hope that this doesn't sound too ghetto, but I would love to have an Old English, if there's one in there."

I must have winced because out of nowhere she flashed and said, "Don't look at me like you're better than I am. You're drinking what you like. Hey, I know what kind of man you are, that's why I never date a man who wears a suit. I mean you guys think that you are the shit, because you drive nice cars and live on the other side of town."

Now what just happened? I had not known this person two minutes and she was already getting defensive. I could tell that she'd been hurt by someone so deeply that anything resembling a male was in trouble. I didn't take it personally. Instead, I searched for her Old English beer knowing that Jennifer was ghetto enough to have one there. Within minutes I handed Tish her beverage of choice.

To avoid being the recipient of someone else's madness, it was time for me to exit. I said, "Tish, here's your Old English. Enjoy your drink. Excuse me, I have to use the rest-room."

There was nothing about her that made me believe she could be my soul mate, and if so, I would declare that mating season was over for life. I had never set out to be anyone's emotional punching bag and I wasn't about to start. I was ready to leave and tried to locate Jennifer. In my search of the place I saw the most stunning young lady I had ever seen in my entire life. There she was just sitting alone, apparently as miserable as I was starting out. But I had already had about three or four shots of Hennessey by then and I was feeling nice.

The first things I noticed were her crossed legs. Her fingers were intertwined and placed in the middle of her lap so that sly admirers, like me, couldn't see between her legs. She was a lady before she ever spoke a word. Her beauty began to arouse my curiosity and a part of me was beginning to feel lucky. She was just sitting there in a small chair near the wall, under portraits of my cousin's immediate family. I was waiting for the right moment to introduce myself. When she turned to look at the pictures a light came on inside my head and my intuition catapulted me across the room.

"That's my Uncle Lester and my Aunt Jesse," I said as she turned around to see who was speaking.

"Oh yeah," she said with a smile. "And who may I ask is this fine young brother I'm looking at?"

"I'm sorry, my name is Shawn Alexander."

While reaching out to shake my hand, she said, "My name is Brooklyn. Pleased to meet you. Well who are the rest of these people, if you don't mind me asking?"

"No, not at all."

Ten minutes earlier I felt like I was headed down a one-way street towards Ignorance-Ville. Somehow faith allowed me to make a u-turn and now I was headed in the direction of Ultimate Satisfaction.

After looking at all the pictures on the wall we danced and laughed into the morning. It seemed like neither of us wanted the music to end. I saw Jennifer and her friend staring at us from the hallway. Renee and Tish, the two ghetto queens from hell, just rolled their eyes as they looked on in disgust. Jennifer hadn't invited Brooklyn. She had come with a male friend of Jennifer's.

"Shawn, can I talk to you for a second?" Jennifer asked as she tapped me on the shoulder.

"Sure you can, but while we're all standing here, allow me to introduce you to Brooklyn. Brooklyn this is my cousin, Jennifer, the birthday girl."

I was so embarrassed, Jennifer never acknowledged Brooklyn. No sooner had I introduced did Jennifer turn and strut away.

"What's her problem?" Brooklyn asked innocently.

"She's probably had too much to drink. Excuse me for a second, I hope that you won't mind waiting for a few minutes."

"No, go right ahead. I'll just wait right here. I understand."

"Shawn, I can't believe you! How could you come to my party and embarrass me this way?" Jennifer asked when I caught up with her.

"Embarrass you? Now how did I do that?"

"My friends told me how you treated them, acting like you were better than them."

"Well, I'm not trying to be funny or anything, but I am. Jen, don't ask me to feel the same way you do about your friends, okay? Can you honestly tell me that Renee and Tish are my kind of girls? One of them is an insecure Old English drinking fool, and the other is a used-up beauty queen."

"Dang, Shawn, that sure is some mean ass shit to say about my girls. They're not that bad are they?"

"Oh yeah. If you were a man, which one of them would you date?" I asked. When she couldn't answer I snapped, "That's what I figured!"

"So, who is the lucky lady?" Jennifer conceded.

"I told you earlier, her name is Brooklyn."

"I wasn't hearing that. My girls were hurting and I was just looking out for them. Tell her that I'm sorry and that I was just tripping. I had a little too much to drink."

"I've already handled that, Jen."

"All right, Shawn. Do you forgive me?"

"Yeah, as family what we have for each other is unconditional. You know that I love you. But please, stop trying to fix me up with your friends. It's never gonna work."

I went back into the living room and Brooklyn was just sitting there looking beautiful, smiling a dangerous smile at me as I walked towards her. "Hey, let's get out of here," I said.

"And what makes you believe that I'm going to leave with you tonight?"

"I just thought that you'd like to get something to eat. And to tell you the truth, I overheard you tell Raymond that it was okay for him to leave, and that you'd be all right."

"Oh, so I guess I'm busted. I hoped that you wouldn't mind taking me home."

"No, not at all. I'll take you anywhere you want to go, just say the word."

"So, tell me Shawn, can you cook?"

"Yes, but I'd much rather eat something that you've prepared."

"I haven't been grocery shopping this week, so there is nothing at my apartment."

"Well, I have something at my place, if that's all right with you."

"I would love to cook breakfast for you. I make screaming eggs and my pancakes aren't bad either."

I was in a zone and everything was working. I had washed my car earlier that day and Brooklyn noticed.

"I see that you are a man who likes nice things. I love a man who takes care of the things he loves and I'm not afraid to do my part either," she said with a smile. After I opened the door for her she reached over and opened up my door for me.

When we got to my house she was overly impressed that I was a homeowner, yet she never once asked me what I did to make a living. Brooklyn was a special young lady, with special obvious talents. She was one of God's most beautiful creations at five-feet seven with a figure eyes could never measure. She was drop-dead gorgeous, yet her soul seemed so humble. She was seductive and had an unforeseen potential to be the girl of my dreams.

"Do you have something that I can put on besides what I'm wearing? I cook better when I'm comfortable," she said.

"Yes, my room is down the hall to your left. I'm sure that you can find something to put on in there."

It was cold, so I had to turn on the heat. I rushed to the CD rack and searched for a song we had jammed to at the party. By the time I had the song playing she had pored me a drink. She had chosen a plain white dress-shirt that I had worn a million times, but she worked it and looked awesome! Her hair was long and flowing. It was an unusual sandy-brown color that matched her skin and blended in well with the color of her eyes.

You could have stuck a fork in my hand and served me a plate of her forever. I was done the very second I saw her and told myself that it was okay to marry her tomorrow if she said yes. It was now or never, a defining moment. I wasn't about to let it slip away. I had been so caught up in my career that I had forgotten about this part of life. She was top of the line, and I knew it. A voice inside of me said, 'Shawn, take your time. Don't blow it.'

Brooklyn handed me my drink and said, "Taste it and make sure that it's okay."

I took a sip and said, "Sure, it's fine."

I turned around on the sofa and began talking to her while she was cooking. She turned out to be an excellent cook and prided herself on paying attention to the small things.

After our meal we sat down on the sofa and held each other for hours. It was Saturday and neither one of us had to work.

"I really appreciate you not trying anything last night, you are truly a gentleman," Brooklyn said. "Most men would have tried to take advantage of me, but you seem different."

"Thanks. I really would like to get to know you before anything like that gets started. I mean, I don't even know your last name. All I really know is that you are a great dancer and a fabulous cook."

"My name is Brooklyn Jana Anderson. I am twenty-five years old and a graduate from Penn State University."

"So what did you major in?"

"I majored in business and minored in Psychology."

"And what kind of work do you do now?"

"I am an administrative assistant at a law firm over on the north side of town."

"That's great!" I was elated to know that she and I had the same interests and background that I just had to tell her a little about me.

"Well, I majored in Psychology as well and I have my own practice. But, enough about me…let's continue with you. What do you like to do when you're not working?"

"I love to run and dance and occasionally I enjoy singing a song or two. More than anything else I enjoy pleasing the man I'm with."

"Are you dating someone right now?"

"I just broke-up with a man who promised to love me forever, only to find out that he was already married and living a double life. I threw away five years of my life and for what?"

I could tell that she was getting ready to cry but somehow she pulled herself together and said, "I haven't been with anyone for over a year now."

"That's understandable," I replied. "To get over something like that takes some time."

"I need to go home and get myself cleaned up and maybe I'll call some of my friends and find something to get into."

"I was thinking that maybe we could spend the day together, and get to know each other. That is if you don't have any other plans."

She looked at me and said, "No. I mean, yes, I would love to spend the day with you. Just take me home and give me some time to freshen up. I'll call you when I'm ready."

Brooklyn and I had a wonderful weekend together. About two months later, after getting to know each other, we both decided that we would start seeing one another exclusively.

My Aunt Jesse kept her promise to me, and often came by my office to visit. One day I could tell that she was dealing with something that was weighing heavy on her mind again. Her son, Little Lester, who we had always called L for short, had gone and fallen in love with a young lady Aunt Jesse called a brainless little nothing. She didn't like to work and was okay with L not working as well. She had three children by three different men and all of the fathers were in jail on drug related charges.

"Lil-Shawn, I don't know what to tell you. L done lost his mind! He quit his job and moved in with Tania, the eastside ho. Now, from what I've heard she has a bunch of ain't-gots. She ain't got no car, she ain't got no money, and from what I've seen, the heifer ain't got no front teeth."

"So what does L see in the young lady, Aunt Jesse?"

"Well, I guess that it's got to be her big butt. You know men always want more than they can handle. It's self-explanatory. She must be pretty good at working what her mother gave her. Why else would all the men on the eastside be running behind her the way they do?"

"Why are you so angry about him dating her?"

"Little Lester has a great heart and he's very loving. I'm afraid that he won't be able to let go. I mean, he's already saying that he's in love with her and he's only known her a month."

"I guess you know what I'm about to ask you, don't you?"

"Honey, I thought that you'd never ask."

"Yes, tell him that I'd love for him and this Tania to come and visit me one day next week."

"Okay, and if I have to bring them myself then, I will. And Lil-Shawn, one more thing. Thank you again for your help turning our bedroom into a Motel-6." She smiled as she walked out of my office.

The next week L and his girlfriend Tania came to visit me. I was surprised to see how pretty she was. I almost thought that Aunt Jesse had been lying until Tania started smiling. She had at least three of her front teeth missing, and a couple of them were gold-plated. My cousin L had gone and fallen in love with a big butt and a smile, and it was my job to help him sort things out.

Tania was everything that a real man didn't need. It's true, she was down for her nigga, but my cousin L wasn't a nigga. He was my cousin in search of true love. He was traveling a dangerous path and come to a fork in the road of life. He needed to know just where he was on his journey. I was his cousin, we were family, and I wasn't about to lie about his present condition. Tania was in search of a drug, which she respectfully calls 'her niggas,' and I wasn't about to allow her to OD on my cousin.

Little Lester, from what I could see, was already willing to sacrifice all his tomorrows for a hit of Tania's fat ass today. Tania shook what her mama gave her and asked for so little in return. She craved nothing but a hard stick and the company of a fool. She liked it rough and wouldn't accept anything less than confusion. She didn't require love, but requested mayhem. She longed to remain connected to this strange illusion and felt that she was put here on earth to be somebody's bitch.

After hearing them go on and on about what they needed from each other, it was clear to me that L was out of his league. Here was a boy trying to play a man's game. Picture if you will, a pure speck of white clay being mixed with the nasty, infected, contaminated dirt of turmoil.

Tania sat there smiling at me and I finally spoke directly to her. "So, Tania, where do you hope to be one year from now?"

Without hesitating she replied, "Alive."

"No, it's more than that, Tania. I want to know what are your goals in life?"

"I don't have no goals to speak of. I just want a roof over my babies' heads, some food, something to drink, and my nigga. That's all. What more can a girl ask for out of life?"

I made it a point to watch L's reaction to the things she was saying.

"What about your children? Don't you want more out of life for your children?"

"Yeah, but they probably gonna be just like their fathers. All of them are hardheaded and bad as hell."

It was time for me to ask L a few key questions. I started off by saying, "Where do you hope to be by the time you're twenty-five, L?"

"You know, Shawn, I want to be successful. I don't want to work hard all my life like my father."

"Where are you working right now?" I asked.

Tania interrupted me and said, "My nigga ain't got to work. I take care of what's mine. I got some work for him to do right there at home."

L was so sprung that all he could do was smile. He couldn't pull his head out long enough to see that he was in too deep. "Yeah, that's right baby, and tonight I'm gone put in some overtime." I cringed.

"What kind of work do you do Tania?"

"Why are you asking all of these damn questions? Are you from the IRS?"

"No, of course I'm not. I'm just a concerned family member who hasn't seen his cousin in a while and I want to see where his head is at. And now I know."

"What do you know?" she asked.

"I know that my Uncle Lester didn't raise his son to be weak. I know that his name is not 'my nigga,' but Lester Johnson. I know that something has happened to L so he feels he cannot become a man with you taking care of him. I know that many of our people are hurting, but that a great deal of the hurt stems from the choices that they have made.

"You see, Tania, I know that you are hurting inside and that you need someone there at all times to share your pain. I know that something or someone has caused you not to believe that you deserve more. I know that you mean well, but you can't see past your pain, so you continue to blame others for your downfalls. How do I know that, you ask? Because, I can hear the things that you don't say. You see, my cousin is unable to see past your anatomy. I have been listening to the souls of this world and know we all must look beyond.

"You have allowed this way of life to sift through your morals and now your soul is lonely and you only desire company. Before I give you something to wipe away those tears, you tell me what I know," I demanded.

I handed her some tissue and asked her to give L and I a few minutes alone. By that time, I felt that she had heard enough and was ready to leave the room of truth.

"So L, what did you hear when she was talking?"

"Man, I know what you are getting ready to say, but that's my girl."

I thought about my next statement for a moment before saying, "What is it about this woman that you feel you need? If you took her butt off, what would you have?"

"Man that's messed-up. Why are you coming at me this way? I thought we was family."

"This is what real family does when he knows his cousin is in trouble. There are times when we are dealt a losing hand. We can tell as soon as we get the cards that we have no chance to win." I knew their chances of having a future were slim to none.

"Yeah, I know what you're saying. I've been dealt some of those hands before myself."

"No, L, your hand is like that now! You can't win playing these cards, my brother. There is one thing different about a card game and real life. In real life you aren't forced to play your losing hand. Being a man is not easy but it has its rewards. Never let anyone tell you that it's okay for you to stay at home and forfeit your right to be a man. I once heard that a man is measured by the amount of responsibility he is willing to accept.

"When you leave here today, go and measure yourself. I've talked with your mother and she is getting the extra room ready, so that you can go back home and get yourself together."

I smiled at him and said, "Hey, L. The next time you go and get yourself a big butt, get a brain to go with it."

"Thanks, I love you, man. Good looking out cuz."

"No problem. That's why they pay me the big bucks. Take care, and tell everyone I said hello."

"Okay, Shawn. Peace."

"Later."

By the time I finished talking to them, I was mentally exhausted. I needed to get home. Brooklyn and I had planned to go to the movies later on that night.

We had vowed to never allow work interfere with our emotional commitment. We became the very best of friends and had started talking about marriage. I thought that everything was going great until later on that same night.

We were sitting on the sofa enjoying the fire after the movie. I gently began stroking her cheek but I felt tears. Brooklyn was crying, and what she was about to say sent our relationship into a tailspin.

"Baby, what's wrong?"

"I'm so sorry," she sobbed.

I had no idea what she was sorry for but I could tell that whatever it was, it was hurting her.

"You have always been there for me, Shawn." She paused and choked back more tears. "I never meant for this to happen."

"For what to happen, Baby? What is it? Just tell me, it's okay."

"No, not this time. Shawn, you are a smart man, but you can't fix this."

"Just try me. Haven't I always listened to you?"

"Well, Baby, do you remember the guy I told you about when we first met?"

"Yeah, what about him?"

"Well, a few weeks ago he called and asked me to have lunch with him. I didn't see any harm in it. I agreed."

"So, why are you crying, Brooklyn?"

"I did something I shouldn't have."

"Okay, so you had lunch with an old boyfriend. I forgive you, no big deal."

"No, Baby, it was more than that. After lunch I went dancing with him down by the pier. On our way home, we got a room and had sex."

I was in shock. Too upset and hurt to speak. Her voice sent spirals whirling in my head. My feelings were too distorted to make sense out of what I had heard. I sat with a blank expression and felt like I had lost a loved one. I couldn't move. Brooklyn betrayed me much like my mother had betrayed my father.

It is amazing how life can sometimes feel like one big circle. Things simply revolve around another, over and over. This must be what my father was feeling the first time he knew that my mother had given herself to another.

"Why aren't you saying anything, Shawn? What are you feeling? Tell me please, what are you thinking?"

I turned to her and said, "Is what I'm feeling really important to you Brooklyn?"

"Sure it is. If it wasn't, I wouldn't have asked you, Shawn."

I sat attempting to gauge my level of composure. The love of my life appeared unwilling to allow me enough time to remove my ego from the equation.

"Brooklyn, I'm gonna need some time to think. So why don't you go home and give me some space?"

"Aren't you even going to let me explain why I did what I did?"

"When I'm ready to discuss why you did what you did, you'll know."

I walked over to the hall closet and grabbed her coat. Brooklyn flinched. Perhaps felt that I was going to throw it at her, but being the gentlemen that I am, I helped her put it on.

"I love you Sh—." Before she could say my name, I placed my hand over her lips, turned her around and walked her out the door.

"Call me. Promise that you'll call me, okay?"

I knew this escapade had nothing to do with sex. Brooklyn needed closure to a relationship that for all intents and purposes, had already been closed. It was obvious she had been in search of something that had nothing to do with sex. She had not been ready for me. She had allowed her mind to be played like a cheap deck of cards, when all she had to do was allow herself to be loved. She wanted to be treated like a lady, so I showered her with affection. Brooklyn could not understand why she had grown so weak in the hour when our relationship should have given her strength. Perhaps she had forgotten that just a few months ago she had been mistreated.

The moment before she gave herself to him, she had denounced all of my efforts to bring joy into her life. There was a part of her that felt incomplete, so she gave up that which she had promised me. She gave herself to another man for a chance to feel forget. What she didn't understand was that there was never an emotional connection between the two of them. Our cries for love aren't always met with accommodating results. So what do we do? We tend to force our morals upon those who have no ability to adhere to its premise.

'Why can't you love me?' is a song that plays forever in the insecure minds of the emotionally needy. Not quite willing to wait for the answers, we simply indulge the

matter until it brings us our results. It is useless to attempt to change what is, and just as senseless to attempt to undo what was.

I allowed her pathetic spirit to rest upon my shoulders without ever asking her how long I would be asked to carry her burdens. Brooklyn spoke of becoming a part of my future, but she had never convinced herself to close the doors to her past. So now I was forced to play the victim role. Within seconds my heart, torn into small pieces, left me to question my ability to make it through the troubled times lying ahead. I had to rebuke the images that had begun to run amok through my conscience.

The decisions Brooklyn had made were not going to deter my quest for happiness. Though, in a great deal of pain, I still had my ability to reason. The way I loved Brooklyn made me vulnerable. Knowing I couldn't love her any other way made the way I felt for her real.

I cried as I stood near the window and watched her drive away. I forced my legs to stand still so as not to stop her from leaving. I hated having to choose between loneliness and deceit. I was going to miss the smell of her freshly washed skin against mine. But just knowing that she had allowed another man to penetrate a vessel that I had promised to treasure, gave me the strength to let go. To me, love is less physical than many people know.

I understand that, at times, we are measured by the trials we have the ability to overcome. Man's strength does not come from the thought of being tested, rather from the test itself. I have never heard of a flower growing without the rain, nor have I heard of someone achieving success without encountering pain.

I was forced to adhere to the very advice I had administered to my clients. They became my lifeline for my emotional stability. Brooklyn and I had often spoken of a forever together, while knowing that realistically we are only given one day at a time.

Brooklyn taught me that her interpretation of forever, was when she became engulfed with self-pity. The U in US turned into the M in ME, and the word, commitment became too cloudy for her to see. Brooklyn had allowed her soul to become caught up in the great web of deception. Until that day, it had never crossed my mind that I would be in this situation.

Brooklyn called me several times daily, leaving messages, which at that moment in my life were in vain. She'd say things like, "I love you too much to lose you this way," and "Isn't there anything I can do to fix what has been broken?" She told me that she loved me with all her heart and soul. Yet I couldn't help but to wonder on the night in question, just how she managed to extract them both as he penetrated her.

While I was dealing with all of the mischief running around inside my head, my sister Tashay called me out of the blue.

"Shawn ,what's up?" she asked easily.

"Nothing. I'm just sitting around here chilling, that's all."

I wasn't the best liar in the world and Tashay could always tell when I wasn't telling the truth.

"Well, Shawn, I am down the street from your place right now and I was just wondering if you want some company?"

"Hey, Tash, you're my sister. You know that you're always welcome."

"Okay, then I'll be right over. I'm going to bring us something to drink and that way maybe you can tell me what's really going on."

Within minutes she was knocking at my front door. I tried to gain my composure, as I knew she would interrogate me.

"What's up, bro?" she smiled when I answered the door.

"Ain't nothing. Just trying to unwind from a long grueling day, that's all."

"Shawn, shut up. You've got that same dumb-ass expression on your face that you did when we were kids. I know you're lying. You know me better than that, so come on with the truth. What's wrong? This is me, your sister. Don't you remember? I studied Shawn 101 growing up and I know a Shawn Alexander lie when I hear one."

Tashay walked into the kitchen and poured us a couple of drinks. "Oh, I see that you've already been drinking, why didn't you tell me that you had a glass?"

"Damn, Tashay. What's up with all the questions?"

"Am I irritating you? It ain't like you see me everyday. Something is wrong with you and I'm not leaving until you tell me."

She slipped her shoes off with the tip of her feet and curled up on the sofa.

"Does this have anything to do with your little girlfriend, what's-her-face?"

"Her name is Brooklyn."

"Yeah, yeah what ever! You know I ain't never really liked her anyway. Brooklyn, Crook-Lyn, it really doesn't matter to me what her name is. What did she do?"

"Just when everything seemed to be going great; she told me something that really upset me."

Tashay wasn't just my sister, she was my friend, and it hurt her to see me hurting. "What did she say?"

"We were just sitting on the sofa, listening to some music. I was holding her in my arms and when I attempted to stroke her cheek I could feel her crying. So I asked her what was wrong."

"So what did she say? Why was she crying?"

"She told me that she needed to get something off her chest."

"Don't tell me that trifling bitch has got another man."

"Well, not exactly, but you're close. She told me that she had lunch with an ex-boyfriend of hers one day and after they ate, they just sat around and talked for awhile."

"Don't tell me, she gave that nigga some dessert."

"Look, Tashay. Are you going to let me tell you what happened?"

"Okay, okay, go ahead."

"Well, she told me," I paused to gather strength, "whatever they said at lunch led them to get a room."

"Shawn, that's messed up. I'm sorry to hear that. I knew the moment I saw her that she wasn't no damn good. What kind of woman would do this to someone she claimed to love?"

That comment caught me off guard and thoughts of Mama's story flooded my head. Before I knew it I responded, "Our mother!"

Tashay choked on her drink. She sputtered, "What in the hell are you saying? Did you just say 'our mother?'

That's messed up, Shawn. Now I know that you're angry. But to bring Mama into this, that's really a low blow. Mama ain't never done nothing trifling like that, has she?"

"Never mind, I didn't mean to say that."

"Oh no, you're not that kind of person. You always think before you say things."

"There are some things better left unsaid and this is one of them. Let me just say that Mama ain't no saint."

"No, you're not gonna get off that easy. Tell me what you're talking about."

"This whole thing started with me talking about Brooklyn. Let's just finish that conversation and call it a day."

"Okay, Shawn. I don't think that you understand what I'm saying. I will hurt you if you don't tell me what's going on," she demanded.

"I really feel like this is neither the time nor place to have this discussion."

"Look don't treat me like I'm one of your confused clients. I can handle anything you have to say."

"Okay, Tash. Brace yourself. What if I told you that practically everything you've being told about our parents was a lie? Are you prepared to deal with that?"

Tashay was pouring herself another drink. "Yes, at this point I'm ready to deal with anything you have to say."

"Tashay, Mama wasn't a loyal woman. She lived a lie, and you are the result of that lie."

"Okay, now quit all of that mumbo-jumbo and tell me what you just said."

"I'm saying that I am your brother and Mom is your mother, but our fathers are not one and the same."

"Did you just tell me that the man I've been calling my father all these years, is not my father?"

"Yes, that is exactly what I'm saying."

She reached out for me with tears in her eyes. I knew her life would never be the same again. There are some questions we must never ask, for the answers may uncover an unbearable truth. Though many of us feel strong, it would shock us to learn how fragile we really are.

Learning that my father was indeed not hers was a dreadful revelation that depleted her. Her once enormously strong exterior was shattered. She clutched a pillow and planted her head firmly against my shoulder. As she cried I could feel her soul being torn apart. I didn't have to ask her what she was feeling. I felt her pain as she searched for the love that I held inside my heart for her. We sat crying for one another as the healing started. We hoped our hearts would never again be forced to tolerate this form of agony.

"Do you know who my father is?" she asked.

"Yes, I know who he is," I answered.

"Well, what is his name, Shawn?" she inquired devoid of emotion.

"Do you remember walking through the mall back in high school, and all of those people were trying to get a guy's autograph?"

"You mean Kenny Morrison? The man that Dad seems to hate?"

"Yeah, him. Well that's your father."

"Kenny Morrison? Are you sure? How long have you known about this?" Tashay asked angrily.

"I can understand you being angry with me. I would be upset with you if you had kept something like that from me."

"I'm not mad at you. You are my brother. I know that you meant well."

"Dad had to have been humiliated by all of this, yet he never loved you any different than he loved me, Tash."

"Don't tell Mama that I found out, okay? I'll tell her in my own time."

It was getting late and Tashay had to be at work early the next day for a telephone conference. So we hugged and said our good-byes. I never really spoke to Tashay again about who her father was. My guess is that she chose to forget the conversation all together.

It was about eleven o'clock when Tashay left my house and I couldn't sleep. I decided to call the strongest person I knew in this world, my father. He was a light sleeper with lots of time on his hands. He was a third degree Mason with wisdom to burn.

I was in dire need of some of his emotional kindling. I loved my father but I had no chance to express to him how much he meant to me. He had a thing about a man refusing to be humble. To him, it was a weakness that steals our opportunity to succeed.

My father had a way of speaking that could pierce your soul and challenge your sense of reasoning. He was a very smart fellow but ever since my mother betrayed him, he had become a loner. He read book after book and never had time for gossip. He became a hermit and though there were times when he came around, his words were forever few.

I needed to inquire about the dramatic journey upon which I was about to embark. Though I often wondered if Dad had ever made it back socially, I was willing to try my luck with whatever part of him had been strong enough to survive. Luckily, I knew I had my father's heart, and knew I had to forgive. I had to forgive Brooklyn before moving on with my life. Calling Dad wasn't the easiest thing I had ever done, but the thought of going through this with his input made dialing his number less difficult.

"Hello, Dad, how are you?" I asked when he answered the phone.

"Is this you, Shawn?"

"Yes sir, it's me."

"It's kind of late, boy. What are you doing up at this time of night? You should be resting that brilliant mind of yours so you can minister to the troubled."

"Oh, Pops, I'm not really sleepy at all. In fact I would like to talk to you about something, if you have time to listen."

"No one has time son, but as long as I'm blessed to breathe, my ears will be at your service," he told me. "I was just about to make a pot of coffee. Would you like to come over and have a cup or two with me? I could use the company myself."

"Sure, I'll be right over. Thanks, Dad."

He lived about fifteen minutes away and I couldn't wait to get there. I hurried and put on the first thing that I saw. I slipped on an old pair of yard shoes, grabbed the keys and was in front of his house in less than ten minutes. I rushed to get out of the car and have a talk with my father that was long over due. Before I could knock he had opened the door.

"Shawn, do you still live over off Jackson and 22nd?"

"Yes, I haven't moved. I still live in the same place."

"Well I've been over to your house several times and I've never gotten there in ten minutes. What seems to be the problem, son?"

How could I just come out and tell my father that my girlfriend had been playing off on me. He knew something was wrong but he wasn't the type of man to speculate. He stood there like a well-schooled chess player, patiently awaiting my next move. He poured himself a cup of coffee and sat down in a chair near the window. The view of the city was spectacular.

"Do you know why I choose this house to live in my son?" he asked me.

"No sir, why?"

"Because of this window. It wasn't the beautiful trees outside, or the secluded neighborhood. No, it was this one window right here."

"What's so special about the window, Pops?"

"Well, you see Shawn, everything has to travel through the light. No matter how dark life gets for us, at some point and time God promised to shine a little light down on us. When I sit in this chair, and look out amongst the lights, I am reminded of the promise He has made to all of us. This window allows me to see past the dark clouds of misery and keeps God's promise forever in reach. I don't understand why you are unable to formulate the words necessary to converse with me, but if it is of my doing, please do forgive me."

His words were meant to convince me and to that point they had not been spoken in vain. My father was a very handsome man and an impeccable dresser. He never really wore expensive clothing, but made sure that whatever donned his body was sleek and clean. He always taught me to pay careful attention to the small things, for he said they would one day become bigger than life.

I stood next to my father drinking a cup of coffee, staring out of the reason he had bought his house. My soul rose to the rim of my mouth, and suddenly I began to speak.

"Today I felt a great pain inside my heart that has humbled me. My girlfriend told me that she gave herself to another man."

My father was forced to speak on a subject that to this day had changed his life forever. A sense of meditation began to hover over the room. What I had just said was about to reopen wounds that for years had been forced to heal through silence. He sat quietly for a minute as he pondered my statement.

Finally he said, "Shawn, I am sorry that you've been betrayed by an emotion that scorns the hearts of so many. We as people were not born to deceive, my son, but when a man breathes the airs of deception he will undoubtedly exhale betrayal. How do you feel at this very moment, Shawn?"

"Like someone has trampled all of my dreams."

"Do you know why you feel so crushed?"

"No, not really. I guess I feel this way because I wanted to believe that she felt the same way I did."

"I have learned that it is unfair for us to assume the thoughts of any man. I have come to understand that words are only as good as the deeds of those who speak them. We must learn that reality can never be challenged."

I felt like he was talking in riddles. "What does that mean?" I asked sincerely.

"Love has blinded so many of us, son. When we are shown the truth we simply try to wipe it away with our emotions. Slowly but surely we shall come to realize that the truth can never be wiped away, no matter how deeply we become attached."

"How do you know so much about this?" I asked.

He had never told me a lie, at least not any that I can remember. Before answering the question he took another sip of his coffee. When he spoke again, he said, "Love has played its games on me as well and not unlike you, I too have been hurt. I have touched the surface of passion only to pull my hands back and discover that my soul had been scarred."

"What happened?" I asked.

"I believed in promises that were spoken from the mouth instead of from the soul. I refused to feel what I saw and never stopped trying to touch that which was never there."

"Do I know this person, Pops?"

"Son, the identities of our enemies are only important if we choose to destroy them or allow their wrong to fester and grow inside our hearts. What satisfaction would you get out of knowing who hurt your father? Are you prepared to avenge my demise?"

He chose not to bring down my mother, no matter how I worded the questions. So I stopped forcing the issue and concentrated on my own situation. "So what must I do? Do you have any advice?"

"Give yourself time to heal and learn to forgive."

"Have you ever forgiven the person that hurt you?"

"Sure, that's how I'm able to sleep at night. I didn't leave her because I didn't love her. I left her because she didn't know that it was okay for her to love herself. This Brooklyn that you're talking about, is she the pretty little girl I met not long ago?"

"Yes sir, she's the same girl."

"Try to put yourself in her shoes and tell me how many times would you want her to forgive you. It would be more than once I'm sure. This type of pain has a way of ratifying itself and no man has ever had the power to derail its destination. I've learned how to focus while I am in pain and over the years I have acquired the tools necessary to out-last its motive. Pain comes to steal our hopes and wash away our dreams but we must never give in to the agony that comes while enduring its premise.

"I feel that it is your hope tonight that I will submit to you my encounters with this great demon. I know that you have come to compare notes, in hopes that you might understand why we were all equally born into this world. Son, no two people shall ever think totally alike. Life was never meant to be fair. There will always be the haves and the have-nots. If we were all right, there would be no reason for wrong.

"I have not acquired these books to fight off the emotional ramifications of life, instead I read them to inform myself of their realities. For years I have heard the mumblings of those who believe that I am going crazy up here on top of this hill. They know that I'm all alone up here with my books. I challenge anyone to become one with themselves before they attempt to unite with someone else. Equality shall never be seen through the eyes of man, for man is selfish by nature and to him relinquishing half of anything is too much to ask."

"But what does that mean, Pops?"

"People are always using words like 'forever' and 'always.' If you stop to think about it, who has the right to promise something that doesn't rightfully belong to them in the first place? As a child I was taught that we are only blessed with one day at a time. If that is indeed true, then please tell me just what does 'forever' mean?

"I stopped using the phrase a long time ago and now I just tell people, 'I'll love you as long as I am able to breathe.' We are territorial beings, who sometimes have the audacity to invite others into an institution that has only room enough for one. The smell that once enticed you may one day become appalling."

"But why is that, Pops?"

"Because we all have been taught that we need a companion in order to become whole. We go out and invite passions into our lives that we will never be able to cultivate.

"Brooklyn is not a bad person, she is in search of something that has eluded her. While reaching for that something she took her hand off of the only person who may ever truly love her in life," he said.

When my father talks, I listen. His wisdom bounces off the walls and demands that I be still. He had a way of silencing us by taking walks around the house between statements. It was his way of allowing the things that he had just said to somehow soak in. I found myself mimicking this tradition.

I got up from the sofa for my own pacing to soak it all in. I noticed the old multi-colored quilt that my grandmother had made for Dad when he was a child. I estimated at least a thousand books on the shelves in a room he had turned into a library. While admiring his collection of various small artifacts throughout his house, I couldn't help but notice that he still kept a picture of my mother up next to Tashay's and mine. They were placed there proudly no doubt by the hands of a gentle man with a kind soul to match.

"I hope that you have received something in the midst of my carrying on," he said in his soft-spoken voice.

"Yes sir, I've learned a great deal tonight."

"That's great, son. Be careful out there in those streets and listen to yourself while you are teaching."

"Okay, Pops."

"Stop focusing on the things that people say and concentrate on those things that they do. For ultimately the truth is told through a man's actions and very seldom through his words."

"Okay, thanks for everything, Dad. I'm glad that I came to see you."

"It is my pleasure, son."

"Do you ever get lonely up here by yourself?"

"No more than you do down there. Don't worry. I have a friend and maybe one day I'll introduce you to her."

"That would be nice, Pops."

"Take care, Shawn, and don't be a stranger."

"I won't," I promised.

He closed the door as I started down the stairs back to my car. As I pulled off I glanced up at a father that seemed to be very proud of his only son. He just stood there waving as I drove off.

Brooklyn never stopped calling and she never stopped trying to convince me that she loved me. One day she placed a sea of roses all around my car and she left a note underneath my windshield wiper that read:

Dear Shawn,

I have wronged the man of my dreams, yet I shall never stop dreaming - not as long as I know that you are alive. It is unfair for me to ask you to change your mind about me overnight, so I am prepared to announce my love for you until infinity has come and gone. I miss the way I feel in your strong arms and the smell of your skin when it's against mine. I miss you watching from across the room as I pretend not to notice you groom. I miss the way you say my name and the gentle things you would do when my skies were no longer blue. But more than anything, I miss you.

Love Always,
Brooklyn

Seeing my father that night was a blessing. It was like having an out-of-body experience. There were moments while he was speaking that I felt connected to his spirit, a spirit that had found peace unlike the world has ever known. Somehow he had learned to love himself so deeply that all matters of this world had become secondary. Just listening to him made me understand how blessed I was to be his child. My father has a heart unlike any I've ever seen and his ability to come to grips with his emotions is remarkable. Though there were times I thought he was having a nervous breakdown, it was then that he had experienced a revelation, which had led him to the doors of emotional prosperity. My father saw people for who they were and not for what he wanted them to be. If I were to ever truly be happy, I would have to adopt that same philosophy.

I wanted what he had, so I took the next couple of weeks off from work and caught a plane to Miami. My best friend, Marvin, lived there and he was always calling asking me to come and visit him. It was time for me to take him up on his offer. Marvin is a great listener and God knew that I needed to talk to someone.

He was excited to hear that I was finally ready to come back to Miami for a visit. I had been once, but too long ago. No doubt things had changed since then. He had some vacation time saved up and my timing was perfect he assured me. After getting off the phone my soul was still dejected, but I felt hope after talking with him. I needed to get away and deal with my own issues. This mental retreat was long overdue and it was my time to tell the truth.

I leaned over the bathroom sink and placed both my hands upon the counter-top. I looked at myself in the mirror searching for the pieces of my heart. There I stood after several years of educating others about the heartaches and heartbreaks of love, forcing myself to make a choice between what I felt and reality.

While looking at myself my soul begin to weep, yet my eyes remained tear-less. My hair was flawless, my clothes though quite conservative were well put together. I was in great shape and my bank account wasn't hurting. I stood there for over five minutes, unable to move, unable to feel anything other than my pain. I had finally come to know the pain that so many have expressed. Suddenly I had gained a newfound respect for those who had already worn my shoes. I stood there helplessly wondering when my soul would stop weeping. and I could actually feel my broken pieces getting smaller.

I closed my eyes, hoping that if I took them off of me, it would somehow lessen the aching feeling. But no matter how tight I closed them, it became evident to me that the period in which it would take for me to be immunized from the pain was completely out of my hands. I was falling apart and attempting to brace myself for the onslaught of anguish that would lie ahead. The emotional recovery bag stored inside my head was filling up rapidly with rage and confusion. The strength that had once flowed freely throughout my body became harder than ever to reach for. Every effort I made was depleting what little energy I had left.

I called my secretary to let her know I wouldn't be in for the next couple of weeks and to forward all of my calls to my answering service. Within twenty-four hours, I was getting on a plane to visit my best friend. He had gone to law school, but never finished because of his obsession for fine women. He is a fast talker with a lot to say, and unlike many people, he seems to know what he's talking about. He is a well-read brother who has always gotten what he wanted.

He is the only child of two well-to-do parents and when all else fails, unlike the average working person, help is always just a phone call away for him. I've often called him spoiled because he's never really struggled a day his life. Marvin lives in a nice condo overlooking the ocean that his parents bought him when he turned twenty-one. It was their way of telling him that he needed to grow up and leave the house, but they still take turns paying the taxes on the condo each year.

Marvin works for a marketing firm and knows a lot about making deals. He could sell ice to an Eskimo. I believe that if he talked to the clouds long enough, he might even be able to get an order for a few hundred gallons of water. People would often say that we were like night and day. He was the only true ladies' man I have had the pleasure to know.

The plane couldn't get there fast enough. A part of me wanted to fly it myself, but it didn't take long for me to end that crazy thought. I ordered a couple of drinks and relaxed as I attempted to watch a movie. Unfortunately it was one you watch because you're not sleepy. But it wasn't long after that, that I fell asleep anyway.

I couldn't wait to see my boy. We had some catching up to do, and man was I ready. No sooner had I cleared the plane's corridor, and there he was.

"Shawn, what's up?"

We gave each other the brotherly hug and did the traditional handshake.

"Boy, you're still looking good, Marvin. I can't wait to hear about all those fine honeys you must have lined up."

"How is the family, you know Mom, Dad and Tashay?"

"Oh, everyone's doing fine."

"Man, is Tashay still married to that brother who's afraid to drive?"

"Yes, they're still married."

"So what's this? I'm good enough to be your best friend, but not your brother-in-law?"

I turned and gave him a serious look. Even with that, Marvin felt that it was time to take one more shot at it and said, "I never wanted to marry your sister, but I did want to hit it."

We hadn't seen each other in a couple of years and I knew that if this conversation lasted five more seconds, I would be re-boarding the plane. I said, "Look Marvin, I came here with a lot on my mind, hoping that we could do like we use to."

"What's that?" he asked, chuckling and shaking his head from side to side. The he repeated, "Man, you know, I should have been your brother-in-law, now don't you?"

"Say man, I told you along time ago that I didn't feel like hearing that."

"Oh, I get it. You want me to cut it with the sister-in-law jokes and get serious." He was finally catching on.

"Yes, that's exactly what I want." We were riding down the strip at the time, and man was the city gorgeous that night.

"You know, I thought maybe we'd get something to eat, have a drink, and chop it up about life for awhile." I remained silent.

"So who went and broke your heart, my brother?"

I didn't want our conversation to start off that way, so I simply pretended not to hear him. Instead I began moving my head from side to side pretending to sing a song that was playing on the radio even though I didn't know the words. When I knew that he was going to be persistent, I pointed at a group of buildings on my left.

"So what building is that over there, man?" I asked hoping to throw him off for the last time.

"Oh, that building there. That's the building you're attempting to pawn this conversation off on."

"What do you mean by that man?'

"Look Shawn, I didn't just meet you. I've known you for years and I know when something is bothering you. If we can't talk about Tashay, we've got to talk about the real reason you came here."

"Okay, okay, you're right. But before we start talking about that, what are we going to eat?"

"Man, I know how much you like that chicken you had the last time you were here. So I got Yolanda, this young lady I've been seeing, to pick up some for us. It should be there by the time we get back to my place. You know that

I've got any and everything you want at my bar, so don't worry about getting your head right."

"Cool that's sounds great. I'm starving. I haven't eaten all day. How long have you been knowing this Yolanda girl?"

"Look, Shawn, before you start sounding like you are at work, let me just say that ain't nothing changed but my address. Don't start trying to analyze my life."

I just laughed and hit him lightly on his shoulder. But I responded by saying, "Man, I left my work at home. I'm just hanging out with my boy."

"Cool, just as long as you understand. You called me at three o'clock in the morning. I didn't call you."

When we pulled up to his condo there was another car in the driveway. I saw it and said, "Man, she sure does drive a nice car."

He looked at me and asked, "Damn, you mean you can see her car from here?"

"Marvin I'm not blind. Hell, the car is sitting in the driveway."

"Hell, that's not her car, that's mine. I don't allow my women to park in my driveway, not even when it's raining."

"I see that you still have a lot to learn." Marvin was a fool and he knew it. Something in his past made him that way and nothing was ever going to change him.

"Shawn, man, what's wrong? Who is this bitch? I ought to fly back to Atlanta and shoot her ass, for messing with my boy like that."

I couldn't do anything but laugh again. He was crazy, just like my Uncle Lester.

When we first walked into his condo, the first thing I saw was a great big beautiful black grand piano sitting on a white polar bear rug. There was a large portrait of him, dutifully placed in the center of the room. There wouldn't be any doubt about who was in charge.

"Marvin, this is nice man."

"Thanks, man, I'm glad that you like it."

"Could you have gotten the portrait any larger?"

"Believe me, Shawn, I tried, but the man said that anything larger than this, it would lose its focus and I couldn't have that. So I settled for this one."

Before I could reach the hallway near the dining area, Yolanda came out of the kitchen to greet us. "Well, hello there, how are you Shawn? Marvin has told me a great deal about you," she added.

"I hope it was all positive."

"Sure, when Marvin calls a man his best friend, it's got to be positive."

Yolanda was a beautiful young lady. She was stunning actually. As she turned and walked back into the kitchen, I tried not to stare at her ass. "Shawn, look at all of that, and guess what? It's firm too," Marvin insisted.

Yolanda heard him and appeared to be embarrassed by his remarks.

"Marvin, that's wrong, you shouldn't put her on the spot like that!"

"Man, she's got the spotlight on her all the time."

"What do you mean by that?"

"Hell, she's a stripper and dances down at the clubs three nights a week. So don't let the smooth taste fool you. Yolanda, where is Candice? I thought that she would be here by now, maybe she got lost or something. You should try to find her," he suggested.

Marvin and I went into a back room that overlooked the ocean. It was a nice sized room, with music, a bar, and the whole works. After fixing our drinks we began to talk. He interrupted our conversation to ask, "Shawn, is it warm in here to you?"

"Well a little," I said.

Marvin got a little fancy on me by taking a remote and pointing it towards the back. The wall moved to the left and disappeared. He turned to me and smiled. "Ain't money a beautiful thang?"

"Man that's nice, when did you have that done?"

"Oh, about a year ago the idea came to me. I called up a couple of people and had it done. I wanted to be able to walk out on to the deck whenever I wanted to, and you know how I get when I want something."

We both took our drinks and walked out on the deck and leaned against the railing.

"So?"

"So what?"

"So, are you going to tell me her name?"

"Yes, her name is Brooklyn."

"Brooklyn, is she white?"

"Damn, how come every time I tell somebody her name they always ask that question?"

"That's easy. It's because the name, Brooklyn, isn't a common name for a black woman."

"Well, what's common?"

"You know, Pam, Teresa, Cheryl, Donna, names like that. Enough about the name. What happened with you and Brooklyn and what has brought you to this point?"

"Man, I really don't know where to start."

"Well, allow me to be you. How long have you known each other?"

"I've known her for a little over a year."

"Wait a minute, let me get this straight. You mean a year, as in one?"

"Yes, one year. Is that odd or something? What are you trying to imply? Are you saying that I was moving too fast?"

"No, I'm just blown away by the whole idea of you moving at all."

"I came here to talk to the only person who would listen and understand my situation. Why am I getting all the sarcasm?"

"Okay, I'm going to listen and not say a word. I want you to tell me everything that happened from the beginning to the end."

I took Marvin back to the very first night that I met Brooklyn. I told him about her past and her boyfriend, and gave him everything in a nutshell. He just stood there listening to me as I went on and on about the ups and downs of our relationship. Every once in a while, he asked me a few questions, but for the most part he allowed me to vent. We took breaks to fix our next round of drinks, and continued to bond as I unveiled my sorrows. An hour or so had gone by before he ever said a word. There were times I spoke and he made noises, seemingly amazed that

I could ever feel the things that I was describing. When I started to repeat myself, then he intervened.

"Man I never knew all of this was happening to you. Why didn't you call me?"

"Everything was going great until all of a sudden it blew up in my face."

"That's the kind of thing that everyone tells me is going to happen to me. But you have never adopted my spirit, and this shit should have never happened to you. I love you man, like you were my own brother."

"From what you've said, you've done nothing to deserve this. But, let's not dwell on this right now. Yolanda has a friend I would like for you to meet. Let's wait until no one else is around and talk about this when we are alone, okay?"

Yolanda seemed fine, but when she introduced me to her friend, Candice, I could hear the song '*Ya'll Gone Make Me Lose My Mind*' playing.

"Hello, you must be that pretty man from Atlanta Yolanda has been talking about?"

"Yes, that's me," I agreed.

I was so high by the time Candice came outside on the deck, if I would have dropped to my knees, I would have broken my legs. I yelled out for Marvin to start the song over. We danced until we couldn't dance anymore. She was about twenty-five years old with nothing out of place, nothing. Her hair was long, but not as long as her legs. When she smiled she made me smile. Like my Aunt Jesse used to say, 'she was too pretty to be called beautiful.' Even if having her were a crime, the man would feel too damn lucky to call the law.

She held my hand and kissed me on my cheek. This made me too weak to control myself, and I didn't want her to stop. The pain of missing Brooklyn was gone. I began to kiss Candice back, and gradually she invited me into her world. "How long are you gonna be here?" she wondered.

"For a couple of weeks," I murmured back.

"I know my way around pretty well. I've been in Miami for over five years and I would be happy to show you the sights," she said. She walked across the room to fix a drink and I was captivated, to say the least. The excitement was agreeing with me and I was ready to live on the wild side.

"So how far do you live from here?" I asked.

"Well, I live closer to you than you know."

"What? Here is what you should be asking yourself. 'Am I going to let her leave here tonight or am I gonna ask her to stay?'"

"Baby, where have you been? I live wherever I am," she said.

"And exactly where are you at this moment?"

"With you, I'm living with you for the moment. I live for the moment, because tomorrow is not promised to anyone."

She grabbed the remote Marvin had used earlier that night. She pointed it towards the door and it closed as she turned her back towards me.

"So let's live." She pulled a string on the side of her skirt and it fell to the floor, along with my face. She reached down to pick it up by straddling her legs wide exposing her white lace g-string panties. She was full of theatrics, and I was ready for the next scene.

There I was hanging out with Marvin, the biggest playboy I knew, smiling at the perks that come to you when a brother like Marvin is your best friend. I was caught up in the moment, staring at Candice like I had just been released from prison. Marvin and Yolanda had already retired for the night. Candice was ready to live. Who was I to try and kill her groove? We kissed like starving animals. Though we hadn't known each other but for a couple of hours we had sex like there was no tomorrow.

She made me feel things I had never felt before. Still to this day I am ashamed to admit what it was I was feeling. The next morning, before Marvin and Yolanda got up, Candice and I were already on the road. She told me she had so many things to show me, that we needed to get a head start.

For the first three days, she showed me the time of my life. Everything came back to sex. The time we stopped to get gas, I had been drinking and needed to use the rest room. I remember closing the door behind me but not locking it. She followed waving her panties in her hand. The next thing I know we're going at it again. For a while there I was almost afraid to stop the car again. I hadn't seen Marvin for almost three days and I felt that it wouldn't be right to spend any more time with Candice until I saw him again.

When we finally walked back into Marvin's place, he and Yolanda were lying on the sofa chilling.

"Well, I thought that you had kidnapped my boy, and that I was gonna have to call the po-lice."

"No, you need to check your boy and ask him who kidnapped who," she replied.

While we were out Candice had suggested, in a roundabout way, that maybe I should loosen up and dress with a little more flair, or style as she put it. So we went shopping and I allowed her to pick out my clothes. It felt funny at first but actually it wasn't that bad. Maybe it was time for a change.

Marvin didn't immediately recognize the change in my style, but after he got a better look he said, "Damn brother, is it that good?"

"Is what that good?" I asked.

"Candice, that's what. Man I ain't never had nothing so good that after hitting it, it would make me want to change the way I dress."

"Damn, come here girl and let me hug you. No, better than that, Yolanda, go over there and hug Candice so that some of that sugar might rub off on you, and tomorrow I'll go shopping."

"You're wrong for that," Candice said.

"No, you're wrong. When my boy goes back to Atlanta, ain't nobody gonna know who he is. When he got here three or four days ago, he was still the most conservative person I know. Now look at him, looking like a new version of R. Kelly."

Marvin was wrong, but when he got on a roll there wasn't anything that anyone could do with him. We just had to let him go.

"Man I've been trying to get him to dress like that for almost eight years and you've done it in less than eight days. Now, that's what I call candy control."

By that time, we were all rolling on the floor unable to maintain our composure. There was nothing I could say. Hell, the man had a point. I had to admit that something had happened that made me suddenly change my mind.

Before I got to Miami, Candice was a work-alcoholic who stripped at night and was an aerobics instructor by day. But something happened to her too to make her feel she could take off and hang with me.

After only a couple of hours back at Marvin's, Candice and I left again. She had me living on the edge and I wanted more. She was unlike anyone I had ever seen on TV or anywhere else for that matter. She was a drug that removed my pains. She was so beautiful, so soft, and so right now. Her warmth was convenient and her touch was satisfying. I loved running my fingers through her hair and watching her eyes dilate. She wore sweet smelling perfume and bathed in imported oils. She was erotically mesmerizing and her aura teased my sense of logic.

Candice was everything that every man in his right mind didn't need. But I had to admit that every inch of my being craved her. I had to try and convince myself that Candice wasn't real. It was the only way that I could let go and experience the moment.

One night in bed she rolled over and asked, "Shawn when are we going back to Atlanta?"

"We? I never knew that you had thoughts of going back to Atlanta with me."

A sudden look of anger and frustration set in on her face and from that point everything changed. She jumped out of the bed and started yelling. "What's wrong with me? You don't think I'm good enough to take home to your mother?"

"No! I mean no, that's not what I meant. It's just that everything is happening so fast. Why don't we just start off visiting each other and see how that works?"

"Sure, Shawn, I understand." The sarcasm was dripping. "The car is okay to drive, but when it's time to make a few payments you want to take it back and say, thanks, but no thanks," she ranted.

There she was, screaming at the top of her lungs, acting like I had just broken a promise to her. She must have felt that if she gave her body to me, she would have a chance to be part of my life forever.

"I'm leaving next week. If you'd like, you can come and visit me," I offered.

She had calmed down and was able to reply softly, "Oh I understand. I just got a little carried away, that's all. I'm gonna go and get me something to drink. Would you like me to bring you something?"

"Sure, Candice. Thanks. Can I have some more of that lemonade? It was great."

"Sure you can, baby. No problem. I'll do anything for you."

Five or six hours later, I became light-headed and started hallucinating. I saw things crawling on the walls. I was hearing strange sounds that I had never heard before. She saw that I was acting differently and said, "Baby, what's wrong, why are you acting so strange?"

She turned the music up and began to dance along side the bed. "Are you feeling okay?"

I could hear her and I had some questions of my own. "No, I'm not. But did you see that?" I managed to ask.

"See what? I don't see a thing." She began to laugh louder and louder. "Where is it baby?" she asked.

"It's right there!" I pointed to warn her. "It's coming towards you!" I started running around the room in an attempt to touch the object that I saw crawling along the wall.

"Damn, Shawn, that is sick! What's wrong? Do you need something to calm you down?" She was staring at me like a dragon blowing smoke out of her mouth and nose.

The smoke enveloped me as she continued to dance and laugh at me: a fool who could not see past her beauty. I had gone against everything I had been taught and everything that I had taught others. The next few hours were the craziest hours I've ever spent on earth. The room started spinning in circles and my life began spinning along with it.

Candice continued her crazy dance in the corner near the window. She was moving to a song I had never heard before. She yelled out over the music, "How does it feel to live in my world?"

I lay there, afraid to speak. My vision became more distorted with every move she made. She never stopped laughing. She waved her hands wildly and said, "Since you won't allow me to live in your world, I'm gonna make you live in mine."

She came closer to me as I sat on the side of the bed, paranoid from all of the events that were taking place. She freely admitted that she had put something in my drink earlier. She took another hit off a joint laced with PCP, placed her hands over my mouth and blew the smoke into my face. I began feeling woozy knew the ticket I had mentally purchased wasn't to ride this roller coaster at all. It was a ticket to hell and I was well on my way. This ride took me up as high and low as I could possibly go. I was so far gone that I felt like my hands were tied.

The drug use went on for hours. I became too weak to refuse her advances. I had smoked my first joint with her, and had hit my first line of cocaine. Candice's life was sex and drugs. She was Miami's greatest untold secret and was leading me towards my earthly destruction. After about four or five more days of being locked up with her, I had become her next victim.

On the same night in question, Marvin and his girl were sitting on the sofa wondering about my strange and lengthy disappearance. Yolanda asked, "Hey, have you talked to Shawn today?"

"No, I haven't, why?"

"Well, I might be over-reacting, but I feel there is something that I should tell you about Candice. One day she told me that she had gotten into some trouble and had to go away for awhile."

"What kind of trouble?" Marvin asked with great concern.

"It seems that she had become obsessed with successful men in the past."

"Look, Yolanda, make it plain and cut to the point."

"One obsession was a businessman out of Memphis. While Candice was dating him she became locked on the idea of marrying him. She held him hostage for over three weeks."

"What? You're just now telling me this?

"Yes, Marvin. But I forgot all about because she assured me she had gotten over her illness. She had gone in to treatment."

"I knew it! I knew it! I knew something was wrong!" he yelled. "She was too damn fine to be by herself. Why in the hell didn't you tell me this before?"

"I thought she was well. Really, I promise, Marvin."

"If something happens to my boy, I'm going to kick your ass!"

"Candice was treated for mental problems, Marvin. She was supposed to be fine on her own again."

"No, that bitch is still mentally ill. Anybody who's willing to mess with my best friend has to be crazy. Call over there and make sure that he's all right. Better yet, when you get Candice on the phone let me talk to Shawn myself."

"Okay, baby, I'm calling right now."

After several attempts with no answer, Marvin told Yolanda to show him where Candice lived.

"I can't wait any longer, you've got my boy over there hanging out with a psycho. Come on. Let's go."

It was about half past one on day five when I first heard something that sounded like a doorbell, but after all of the drugs nothing was really clear. Marvin saw Candice's car parked in her stall and knew that we were inside. Since she didn't answer the door he walked around the building and begin beating on the window. Still there was no response.

He walked back to the front door and said to Yolanda, "If someone's in there, I'll bet they come to the door now." The pounding continued.

Candice finally woke up. I was too damned ashamed to move. All I could do was try to touch my face to make sure it was there.

Candice opened the door in her robe. "Hey, what's going on? How are…"

Marvin moved her aside before she could finish. He roared through the apartment looking for me. "Shawn! Shawn! Are you in here?" I could hear him yell.

I was hoping to get myself together before he found me, but I was hung over from one of the most horrific binges ever. There I stood in the middle of the room, looking helpless and pathetic. I was wearing her panties and another pair wrapped was around my neck. There was crusty sleep in the corners of my eyes and I had cocaine residue around both of my nostrils and the ridge of my mouth.

When Marvin saw me, he could tell I was hurting. I lost what little dignity I had left and reached out to him. I sobbed in his arms, "Marvin get me out of here," I begged. "She's crazy!"

"I didn't know Shawn, I didn't know," he murmured as he tried to console me.

Marvin found my own clothes in the closet and helped me get dressed. We ignored the Miami wardrobe, as we both knew I wouldn't be needing those clothes back in my world.

On my way out of Candice's apartment I looked over at her, hoping to get some kind of response. She just sat there motionless and never said a word.

Marvin turned to Yolanda and said, "Are you just gonna stand there and let that bitch disrespect my best friend, or are you gonna handle this for me?"

"What the hell is she gonna do to me? She ain't nothing," Candice said defensively.

Yolanda turned to her and threatened, "You know I've got to whup your ass now, don't you?" She took her earrings off and tied up her hair. Three seconds later the whupping commenced.

Marvin looked over at me and winked. "Now that's what I'm talking about! Shawn, this calls for a beer. Is there any in her refrigerator?"

Now I was sure this was not the world I wanted to live in. There I was watching Candice get beat down, while Marvin searched for a beer. Yolanda and Candice continued going at it in the living room. Pictures and lamps were flying. The couch was dismantled. Yolanda put Candice's robe over her head to blind her, and then beat the hell out of her.

I stood there watching, debating whether I should stop them or get myself a beer. I decided to get a beer myself.

On my way to the kitchen I could hear Candice grumble, "Bitch, I'm gonna kill you!"

But Yolanda was getting the best of her and continued her tirade. "I've told you so many times before, you ain't gonna make me lose my man. You've been working to earn this ass whupping and now you're getting it!"

Candice tried to get away after Yolanda busted her up side the head with a hard right. She was crawling towards the kitchen when Yolanda grabbed her by the ankle. She dragged her body scraping across the carpet. I could imagine the sting of the carpet burns.

Yolanda had skills and she was handling her business Marvin pointed out. Just before Yolanda could bang Candice's head into the coffee table, Marvin said, "Hey, that's enough. Let the bitch go. She ain't worth killing. It won't be long before she kills herself anyway."

"Yolanda baby, now that's an impressive ass whupping you put on her. Don't be trying none of that while you're over to my place," he warned as he used a paper towel to wipe blood off the corner of her mouth.

Yolanda looked over at me and said, "I'm so sorry Shawn."

"Oh, it's not your fault in any way." It was Candice's lack of remorse that made me feel inadequately stupid. But I must admit that a part of me felt vindicated when I saw her lying on the floor holding her side as we walked out the door.

When we reached Marvin's place and I had a day to recover, he and I finally finished having our talk. Out on the deck Marvin started the conversation.

"My brother, you were off the hook. I've never seen you this way. Where do you go from here?"

"Up," I answered. "I have nowhere else to go but up. I have definitely seen the bottom."

"I'm sorry it all turned out this way," he said.

"Don't be. I've learned some vital lessons. No, I didn't want to learn this way, but I learned all the same. I now know that I am in love with a beautiful woman in Atlanta. I must forgive her as God has forgiven me. We all make choices. Some good, some bad. But they are choices all the same. Just as I'm getting a second chance, so must I offer another person the same respect."

"What are you saying, my friend?"

"I am saying that we all fall short sometimes. It is through the grace of God that we're given an opportunity to right a wrong. Over the past two weeks I have been in places I've never dreamed of. I have done things that I am embarrassed to discuss, all because I was trying to outrun these feelings that are inside my heart. I wasn't smart enough to know that I couldn't lie to myself.

"I changed the way I dressed and tried to adapt just so that I could fit in. Look at me now. My soul is hollow and my spirit is weak."

"Damn that's some deep shit you're saying. Where is all of this coming from?"

"It comes from a place inside a man's soul found only after he has been able to come to grips with the truth. It comes from admitting that I'm bigger than my last mistake and greater than the enemies who challenge me. I have somehow made it through the fires of madness. Whether you believe it or not Marvin, I owe it all to you."

My studies tell me that none of us are ever exempt from the pains of this world. I've learned that our boundaries are gauged by our convictions. I learned how to tolerate the mishaps of man, by acknowledging first that we are all human.

After my conversation with Marvin, I checked my messages for the first time since being in Miami. There were several unwanted messages from miscellaneous people and businesses I skipped over. There was only one voice I needed to hear, and Brooklyn had left several messages. One in particular stood out.

"Hello Shawn, this is Brooklyn. Remember me? I'm the one who broke your heart. I know you said that you needed some time, but I pray that you'll forgive me one day and allow me a chance to make it up to you. My phone numbers haven't changed and whenever you decide to call, I will be there. I promise. Call me if you need a ride from the airport. I love you."

I couldn't wait to call her. I needed to know that she was okay. The phone rang three times and I was about to hang up when Brooklyn answered. "Hello," she said in her sweet voice.
"Hello, Brooklyn. This is Shawn."
There was a long pause before she asked, "Shawn, is this really you?"
"Sure, were you expecting someone else?"
"No, never. I never want to hear from anyone else again for as long as I live. When are you coming home?" she asked hopefully.
"Tomorrow at 8:00 pm. I would like for you to be there when I step off the plane."
"Don't worry. If I have to, I'll spend the night at the airport to be on time. Oh Shawn, I love and miss you so much."
"I've been doing a lot of thinking, Brooklyn. I feel that it's time we sit down and talk," was all I could say.

"I'll be there. I promise."

When I got off the plane, Brooklyn was there. She wore a sundress I had bought her awhile back. She smiled at me like I was a king and she was my proud queen. When our eyes met we became whole. Her fear of losing me began healing my emotional wounds. I could feel the harmony that once brought us together.

"Shawn, is it okay to hug you?" she asked meekly.

"No. No, it's not okay unless you plan to hug me forever."

I was down on my knees with a ring in my hand. She looked down into my hands and said, "Oh Shawn, yes, yes!"

We stood there embracing one another in the midst of all our trials. I knew that she loved me and I had no doubt that I loved her.

"Shawn, I'm so sorry," she said, weeping tears of joy. "I promise to never hurt you again."

"Brooklyn, I'm sorry too. But there is no need to promise anything. Just try as hard as you can to make us happy."

Six months after that we were married.

We are now two of the happiest people in the world. She is my Visa card and I don't leave home without her. In fact, we decided to go into business together, and are truly inseparable. We opened a relationship development center and are attempting to build and bring marriage.

Brooklyn and I work well together because we believe in each other. We understand that nothing lasts forever, so we have taken the word 'forever' out of our vocabulary. We now believe that the word is heavily misused. It would be nice to love and cherish someone forever. But the irony of it all is who among us will ever really touch 'forever?'

Brooklyn and I teach our clients to treat each other with love and respect. We assist them in weeding out selfish things that interfere with marital growth. We show them that harmony is not something that one hopes for but rather what he or she works towards. We have teamed up to help mend severed hearts. We teach our clients to aggressively apply affection to the words they speak. It is our hope for our love to become a light that shines brightly enough to lead the rest of the world out of emotional bondage.

We continually try to connect our desires to some form of reality. There is nothing wrong with dreaming, but while awake we must never cease in our efforts to bring our dreams to consciousness. We must never allow our minds to ponder things that have the power to disconnect us from our realities. To do so would put us in total violation of the first law of nature, self-preservation.

We remember that love is powerful, an attachment that can unify hearts but it craves emotional reassurance. Love can be warm, but not all people require warmth in their life. Love can become such a need, but seldom does a needy individual attract a giving soul.

My mother has finally let go of her guilt, and my father still sits by the 'reason' he bought his house on the hill. To this day, he continues to amaze me with his emotional resolve. Tashay never told my mother she knew who her real father was, and something tells me that she never will.

She is still married to Johnny, the man of her dreams, and continues to pick him up like clockwork everyday from the train station.

Aunt Jesse and I still converse from time to time. She and Uncle Lester and have reinvented the light. It is so bright at night around their house it almost looks like a landing strip.

My Uncle Benny messed around and did it. He married himself a black woman and proudly wears her arm around him every time they attend a family function.

Marcus Dewayne, a.k.a. M.D. messed around, caught the Holy Spirit, and is now an ordained minister! Uncle Joe finally got married but his wife doesn't have a sense of humor! Uncle Junior never grew up and as for Little Lester, well he's not little anymore. He weighs nearly three hundred pounds now, and hasn't moved out of that room his parents cleaned out for him over ten years ago.

My cousin Jennifer married an abusive man and feels the need to justify his behavior. She's now always fully clothed but it's not because she has suddenly become shy. It might just have something to do with the bruises she doesn't want us to see.

Marvin finally got married to Yolanda, and they have a beautiful little girl named Jade. Candice wasn't so fortunate. She was found in her apartment, dead from an overdose. The coroner said there was an especially strange aspect of the sad scene. She died with a smile on her face.

Brooklyn and I now have two lovely children: a girl, Brook, who is now seven and a half years old; and a boy I proudly named Lyn, who just turned six. Together they spell the most beautiful name of them all, whether they are white or black.

We have learned to focus on the solution, rather than concentrate on the deed. We were not born to stand in judgment of our people. But rather we were born to teach them how to stand while being judged via emotional compliance. The work that we do is endless and our client base is perpetual. Our success is because Brooklyn and I know 'what happened to forever.'

Four Boys And A Girl

*I*t was just a few days out of the summer of seventy-seven and into the cool days of fall. The Average White Band was just as hot as the O'Jays and Earth Wind and Fire. The three bands were running neck and neck on the top twenty charts that season. We all wore Afro's, Jerry Curls and wide leg pants called elephant ears. It was back when an eight-track was the coolest thing spinning and NaNa was the finest girl on our block. Back when anyone could listen to just about everything that played, and our parents didn't have to check the albums for a censored label. House parties were as popular as today's B.E.T. and thrown more often than Stevie could wonder or Michael could beat it.

NaNa, Bobby, Blue, Tino, and I were the very best of friends. But Tino was always trying to break our cardinal rule: never sleep with a friend. We had all been in some type of trouble: from breaking and entering, to Bobby's specialty, stealing car stereos. No matter which one of us did it, it was still trouble all the same. We had our little problems, but we swore to get through our senior year together if nothing else. We were all tired of being the child in the family who was labeled 'the mess up,' so we decided to stop doing the little things that kept us alienated from the rest of our families. We were three boys and a girl who grew up the only way we knew how: hard.

NaNa, whose real name was Nicole, was the prettiest girl you'd ever see, but there was something about her that we never understood. We never could get past how fine she was, to get to know the real her. NaNa's smooth brown skin was the color of a Nestle chocolate bar and her full body was given to her many years before her time had come to embellish it. She was a tomboy and played harder than most boys. Many times she put us to shame.

Her mother was an alcoholic and none of her siblings had the same father. Almost every night she'd drink until she'd blackout, and she was the worst kind of 'ho' imaginable. A cheap 'ho' that would have sex for a fifth of gin. Most every guy within a five-mile radius had already had her. As the oldest, NaNa was forced to raise her two sisters. To this day they still think NaNa is their mother. We all did our best not to mention NaNa's mother around her.

One day before school started the five of us were hanging out in the street when we heard a sound coming from a dumpster. We rushed over and much to our surprise saw Miss Green, NaNa's mother. She had been drinking and thought she had thrown some money in the trash. I helped pull Miss Green out of the dumpster. NaNa gave her mother five dollars for a bottle of gin and whispered, "Mama, this is so humiliating. Why are you doing this to me?" The fact that we were there as witnesses compounded her pain.

My mother wasn't any different. She was always bringing home some old tired ass nigga, shushing him at the front door, having him take off his shoes. The walls were so thin throughout the building we lived in that you could hear my mother moaning like a cow. The men she chose usually only had five hard strokes in them before they both fell off to sleep. So there never was a real need for them to take off their shoes.

Anyway, Bobby 'Big-Head' Patterson was the jokester in the bunch, and because he was the most unattractive in our little clique, he tried hard to keep us laughing hoping we'd ignore his looks. That's right, Bobby was hard to look at. His head was almost twice the normal size, but no one dared talk about it. Bobby was good with words and could talk about the sun and make it go down. Sometimes, just so he could Jones on you, he'd walk outside with his hair uncombed, hoping to draw attention. If someone, anyone commented, man, he talked about them until they almost cried. Bobby had a thing for NaNa, we could tell. Out of all the times NaNa laid into him about being so ugly, he never once took a shot at her mother.

Bobby, had a problem that had become hard to control. He couldn't go past a parking lot at night, without attempting to take at least one car stereo. I was the talker out the bunch, so I was appointed to always be the distracter. My job was to keep the victim busy while Marvin, NaNa, and Bobby did their thing. Blue would never come. He seemed to always smell trouble and was never around when we'd all got that itch for trouble.

It was fun to live on the edge, and man did we. We loved to take from the rich and keep it for ourselves. Sometimes we'd just take off and get in trouble just for the hell of it. Our parents weren't really concerned with our whereabouts. Blue could smell trouble and disappeared when we got that itch. We'd call him names and say mean things to him, but our words never swayed him to stick around. Blue wasn't the sucker. The rest of us were.

Blue was the nicest guy anyone could ever meet. He was a little over weight. Hell, that's a lie. He was just plain fat. Fat and softer than Charmin tissue. His mother was a dreamer, who didn't stay awake long enough to understand reality. How she ended up keeping her house next to us in the projects we'll never know. Sometimes we joked that Blue's father had to be Bobby. The man who took part in Blue's conception had to be ugly to have made it with his mama. Whatever happened to get Blue's mama pregnant had to have taken place in the dark.

Tino, a.k.a. Big-Dog, was a man amongst boys. He was the toughest person I had ever seen. I looked up to him and stayed on his good side at all times. His two older brothers both seemed to be afraid of him. He was about six-five and weighed over two hundred fifteen pounds. He had been angry since childhood, but nothing about his future was going to stand in his way. At the age of eighteen he had a man's physique and his voice was deeper than most of our fathers'.

Tino's dad was the epitome of a family man. He was home to raise his children and in our neighborhood that was rare. He was a teacher, a well-spoken man with peace in his voice. He demanded the best and accepted nothing less than maximum effort. His only trouble was finding a woman who didn't mind taking care of his three bad boys.

All of us lived in single parent homes, but we never really spoke about missing our mothers or fathers. We had made an unspoken vow to never solicit the mental reigns of misfortune. We all knew there was something that everyone of us simply didn't want to talk about. Why our absent parents weren't there to help support us was at the top of each of our lists.

My name is Roland Maintrain and they all called me Pretty Boy. I had the brains and I was good with the ladies. That's why Tino hung out with me. Even though he was massive, he wasn't the brightest.

NaNa broke our vow one day while we were walking from the corner store.

"Pretty Boy, did they tell you what happened to my father?"

"Well, I was told by the neighbors when we moved in, that he was shot," I admitted. "But we don't have to talk about this."

"You can't tell anyone what I'm about to say, okay?"

"Okay," I promised. "What happened to your father, NaNa?

"Yes, Pretty Boy, he was shot. I shot him. I shot him in the back when I was twelve years old. Early one morning and he came into my room to violate me, like he had done so many times in the past. He wasn't my real father though. My father died from cancer when I was about two and a half. Like my mom, my stepfather was an alcoholic. Sometimes they would be drinking in the living room late at night and he'd wait until she blacked out. Then he'd come into my room and start feeling on me."

"What? No!" I was disgusted.

The boys and I never thought we would see NaNa cry, but she did then. We stopped and leaned against an abandoned car. I held her in my arms as she cried.

"You don't have to tell me anymore if you don't want to, NaNa," I assured her.

"No, I have to. You see, it's been killing me to keep it inside all these years." She gathered herself and continued.

"He came in the room at about three or four in that morning, smelling like a gin factory. I always felt like my mother knew about me being molested. Some of her drinking was probably her way of dealing with that knowledge.

"That morning I took justice into my own hands. Months earlier I had gotten a gun from Big Floyd down the street with some babysitting money. It had been sometime since he had come into my room, but I kept the gun on the side of the bed. It was there against the wall, ready for the next time he came to have his way with me."

"Ah man, that's messed up."

"Yeah, but wait." She paused to deliver the details. "When he came in the room, I lit a candle and smiled, turning the covers back for him. He was so stupid. He thought I had given into the idea of it all. I guess he thought he had screwed me into submission.

"He was smiling like it was Christmas morning and he had just seen his gift underneath the tree. But what he didn't know was that he was getting ready to die." I could see atonement in her eyes. She had my undivided attention.

"While he took off his clothes I reached over the bed and got the gun. I thought I might give him one more eye full before I killed him, so I took off my bra.

"He said, 'That's right, it's about time you stopped fighting it. You're fine as hell NaNa. Take off your panties,' he instructed me.

"'No, tonight I'm going to let you take them off,' I said.

"He smiled and climbed on top of me and asked, 'How does this feel?' As he looked up, I stuck the barrel of the gun inside his mouth and asked, 'How does this feel?'" His eyes were bucked wider than I had ever seen."

"Well, what did he say then?"

"Nothing. He said nothing. As he tried to scramble off of me I shot him in the back."

"NaNa, I'm so sorry."

"Thanks, Pretty Boy. Thanks for listening, but it's all a part of life I guess. I mean there are givers and there are takers, and he got his in the end.

"So what did the police say?"

"I guess it could have been worse. They locked me up in a juvenile detention center for about eight months. My mother finally came clean and said that she had known about the abuse for sometime."

"NaNa, that's crazy."

"Yes, I know. She claimed while he was molesting me, she was too high to stop him. So they released me and threw the case out of court. My stupid mother still tells me to this day that I didn't have to kill him. The worst part is that she feels it was all my fault."

"And what do you say to her, NaNa?"

"Do you want to know how I really feel? Sometimes I wish I had killed them both. Him, for actually penetrating me, and her, for knowing and never trying to stop him.

"I was just a child when it all started. I was forced to think like a woman. He took something from me I'm never gonna get back. I find it hard to trust anyone. Being a girl ain't all it's cut out to be. Anyway, I don't want to talk about it anymore. It makes me sad and right now I don't want to feel sad."

"Okay, this conversation is over. I will never speak on it again," I reassured her, "but I'm glad you told me."

There were a lot of things that we will never forget. But the funniest of them all happened after a party over on the other side of town just two days before we started our senior year.

Tino had a thing for NaNa, but she never gave him the time of day. After what happened that night, he would undoubtedly get the opportunity he had longed for. On our way home Tino took a leak on the side of a building. A loud noise like gunshots made him turn abruptly. We accidentally found out that his Johnson didn't match his body size.

I can remember NaNa yelling, "Dang, Big-Dog, where is it? I know you've been after me all this time, but that was all you were packing? What were you going to do, tickle me?"

That had to have been one of Tino's most embarrassing moments.

Big-Dog replied, "That's messed up, NaNa. It's just cold out here, that's all."

I wanted to say something in his defense but it was seventy-five degrees out that night and Big-Dog didn't have a leg to stand on. Just when I felt things couldn't get any worse, it was Bobby's turn to Jones on him.

"Damn, Dog. You're so small you need a light to find that bad boy. You better do something before you start leaking out of your stomach."

NaNa spoke right up, "Bobby, that's messed up man. How could you say something like that?"

Bobby replied, "Come on, weren't you watching the whole thing? The only reason you're not laughing is because it was so small, and you almost missed it. You know darn well it's not cold enough out here for somebody's Johnson to disappear while he's holding it."

We all laughed and resumed our walk home.

On the first day of school as we were entering our senior year, we all met on the corner of 14th and Mission before walking down two blocks east, to the corner of 16th and Jefferson. That's where the bus generally picked us up. Come with me as I take you on the ride of your life…

We all thought it was going to be just another typical first day of school, but things transpired that changed our lives forever. Ronnie, a.k.a. Trouble, was a well-known rebel whose parents just happened to be well off. He wanted to hang out with us, but his illegal activities crossed the line. He was known for hitting little old ladies over the head and taking their purses in broad daylight.

That morning I saw him walking down the hall trying to get at some girl when our eyes made contact. "Hey, I've got a ride. We can go and get some burgers at lunch time if you want," he offered.

I told everyone about it when we met in the hall after first period. We all decided to go. We never did anything without each other and we weren't about start.

Around eleven-thirty, NaNa, Bobby, Tino and I left with Ronnie in his roomy, blue, four-door Chevy. We were full of ourselves. Blue didn't come with us. He said later that he couldn't get in touch with his mother, but we all figured that would be the case.

Bobby sat in the front with Ronnie. NaNa, who always insisted that I sit between Tino and her, was in the back seat on my left. I was doing my duty as middle rider and Tino was on my right. He and Bobby were getting high and wanted us to join them, but we were practically the only seniors who didn't smoke anything. They would purposely blow the smoke in our direction in an attempt to give us a contact.

Ronnie pulled up to a corner store near to get some cigarettes. "I'll be right back," he said, and left the car running and the music blasting.

An old man was leaning against the wall outside the liquor store. He stared at the car as if he was offended by the loud music. It seemed odd that he never stopped looking into the car.

Bobby rolled down his window and began to Jones on the man's shoes. "Hey, there old fellow. Where in the hell did you get those shoes you're wearing? The heels are so run over they make you look bowlegged," he jabbed.

The man thought that it was funny as well. He laughed while Bobby was talking about him and said, "No, you bigheaded, bullfrog looking idiot. Do you really want to know how my heels got like this?" He explained, "Well, I was doing your mama doggie style and her butt was so wide that while trying to keep my leverage, the pressure from all the strokes made my heels run over."

We all laughed. Everyone except Bobby that is. He didn't expect the man to be able to Jones back.

I said, "Damn, Bobby, that was funny."

"Ah shut-up, Pretty Boy." But he was holding his laughter in knowing another comedian has gotten the better of him. Tino laughed so hard that he choked on his smoke.

All of a sudden, Ronnie ran towards the car. We knew something was wrong. He was breathing hard, and had a crazy look on his face. When he jumped into the car he held his right side tightly. We saw the old man run into the store.

I shouted at Ron, "Trouble! What in the hell did you just do?"

He calmly replied, "Nothing, man. That white man in there was just crazy. He called me out of my name, so I shot him."

Bobby asked, "Man, is he dead?"

"I think so. I mean I don't know! Who gives a damn? We're out of here!" He jammed the car into reverse and then into drive.

"Stop this car, fool!" Bobby commanded. His face grew numb and his high came down faster than Carl Lewis could run the hundred-yard dash. He screamed, "You are crazy, Ronnie! I haven't even had sex yet and now I'm on my way to jail, to become somebody's girlfriend!"

No sooner had we pulled out of the parking lot than the police were behind us. We were now involved in a high-speed chase heading towards our neighborhood. We weren't three blocks away and if we could make it there, our chances of getting away were good. NaNa and I held hands and I remained calm for her sake. Ron seemed to be losing more blood by the second.

Tino finally said, "Ron if we get out of this, I'm going to hurt you real bad!"

What were we going to do? Pull over and claim we knew nothing about what was going on? We had two old-school, twenty-dollar bags of weed inside the car, and a white man dying on the floor in a liquor store. Damn, we were up shit creek and it started to stink.

I shouted, "Ron, pull this damn car over!" But who was I fooling? We were five black kids with petty mile-long records. We couldn't stand to be caught up in this kind of madness. We all knew this crime could take away our freedom forever.

Hell, being accused of robbery was bad enough, but to compound it with murdering a white man was a death sentence. Sure, we were just along for the ride. But prison was full of fools just like us.

Bobby made jokes even while the police were chasing us. "Damn man, all I wanted was a burger!"

I reared back as far as I could and slapped him in the back of his big ass head. "Nigga, it ain't time to be funny. This shit is serious," I chastised.

"Man if you hit me in the back of my head again, I'm gonna seriously lose my mind."

NaNa shouted, "Shut up! Shut up! Let's keep ourselves together and fight later, okay? And Big-Dog, throw that mess out the car! You crazy or what?"

"Hell no," he replied. "Hey, if I'm gonna go to jail, I'm going to get there as high as I can."

Ron shouted, "Don't worry, I'm going to get you all out of this."

He quickly turned down an alley in our neighborhood. There was an opening between some buildings that we had used on other occasions to avoid the police. Ron headed towards it and made a quick left to turn the car sideways.

He shouted, "Go, get out of here!"

We got down as low as we could and made it through a crack in the wall. We ran like the wind towards our apartments. We ran like runaway slaves two minutes from freedom. As soon as we could, we separated, the way we always did. Police sirens could be heard nearby and the sound was closing in.

NaNa yelled to me, "Go! Go! I'll call you later!"

I had never seen Bobby move so fast. His stride lost its form and he became a part of the wind. All you could see was the bottom of his feet and the back of his big ass head, that was getting smaller the faster he ran. He lived farther away than any of us, but did his best to make up the distance.

Tino lived the closest and was the first to disappear. NaNa, being the tomboy that she was, ran almost as fast as I did. But the fear of being caught seemed to give me what I needed to beat her home. I wasn't inside for more than ten minutes before the phone rang. The first call came from Bobby.

"Damn, man, what took your ass so long to get home? I've been calling you for five minutes."

"Shut up, and let me think," I said.

"Well," said Bobby, "what in the hell are we going to do?"

"I don't know Bobby, just chill for a moment." I thought quickly. "Okay, meet me in the back of 'Mama's House' in one hour. Don't let anyone see you."

I hung up the phone and called NaNa as fast as I could and told her the plan.

I called Marvin's house next. He was scared to death, "Man, I did something real stupid."

"What, Big-Dog? What else could possibly go wrong today?"

Big-Dog started off by saying those famous three words that always seem to be followed up by 'stupid.' "Well, you know…"

"No! Big-Dog, I don't know. Why don't you tell me?"

"Pretty Boy, you know I've always wanted a gun of my own. So when we were all getting out of the car and staying low, I noticed the gun that Trouble used just lying on the floor of the car and I took it."

"Please, tell me you're lying."

He had no reply. Silence was Big-Dog's way of confessing.

"Damn, we are through! You know your prints are now all over that gun?"

"Pretty Boy, the gun was so shiny. Before I could think I grabbed it and put it in my pocket." His voice was turning to a whimper.

"Where is the gun now?"

"Right here, with me."

"Bring it with you. Make sure no one sees it. Meet me in the back of 'Mama's House' in fifty minutes."

"Okay, okay, Pretty Boy. I'll be there. Hey man, I'm sorry."

"I know, I know. Just meet me there, bye."

I called 'Mama's House,' a soul food restaurant owned by an ex-con everyone called Mama. She spent over thirty-three years in the state-penitentiary, and was as street-wise as anyone could be. We all went there to cool off when things got hot. Mama had an old school bus she had converted into a hideaway place for times like these. It was parked under an old tree and from a distance the bus looked abandoned. One of the headlights hung down and the left front tire was flat. But when you stepped on board, the inside blew you away. Mama had that old bus decked out so any runaway would think they were staying in a hotel.

Mama said, "Child, what have you kids done now?" Before I could answer she continued, "No, that's all right, not now. I'll talk to you when you get here. You know where to go. I'll leave the keys in the same place."

By the time we all reached 'Mama's House,' the story had hit the news. My first thought was to turn ourselves in. But who was going to believe us? Our lives were messed up, and to compound all the madness, Tino had the gun.

Bobby, forever the comedian, lead off by saying, "Hell, I've got some weed, let's just smoke a joint and think about this later." We ignored him for the moment.

I went behind an old Ford parked near the bus. I pulled down the license plate to reveal the gas cap and found the key to the bus. When we were all safely inside I motioned to Big-Dog to tell the rest of the gang the news.

Ron had been caught and apparently had given our names to the police before he died. A news report said we were wanted for questioning. Ron had told the police that we were in it together. Blue was arrested and was shown on the news being placed in the back seat of a police car. They had a picture of the store owner too, and reported that he had died.

Honestly, I didn't think Ron lived long enough to rat on us. We later learned it was Blue. That scary no good fool revealed our names and the man in front of the store picked us out of some school photos

"Hey man I messed up real bad this time," Big-Dog confessed when he finished his report.

"Damn, Big-Dog, what did you do now?" Bobby asked.

"Well, I took Ronnie's gun from the car."

NaNa was livid. "What? You did what?" she yelled.

"You, big moron," Bobby said. "After all we did to get away from the police, you took a gun that would lead them back to us. Now I know it's time to smoke."

Shortly, there was a knock on the bus door that only I could detect. It was Mama.

"Well, what in the hell have you four gotten yourself into now?" she inquired.

I replied, "Well, Mama, we were only going to get a burger when Trouble stopped at the liquor store for cigarettes. The next thing we knew, he was running towards the car like a bat out of hell. He had robbed the place and shot the store owner."

Mama replied, "Child, that's not what they reported on the news. They said that this was a robbery gone bad and that you were all in it together."

"No, Mama," NaNa assured her. "We knew nothing about what Trouble was planning to do."

"I really don't know at this point," Mama said. "I need to make some phone calls and check with some of my people."

"Wait Mama. There's one more thing." I hesitated but knew she had to be told. "Big-Dog grabbed the gun that Trouble used to rob and kill the store owner."

Mama replied, "Big-Dog, tell me that you weren't stupid enough to do such a thing?"

Tino said, "Yes Mama, I was…I did it."

"Baby, what were you thinking?" Mama asked.

"I guess I wasn't, Mama".

"Well, you've got that right. Child give me the gun and sit down. No one will ever see this gun again." She continued, "I don't want any of you to move. Keep the talking down and remember to listen for my knock," she ordered. I'll help you kids get out of this mess, don't worry."

She took the gun with her and it was never seen again. She had a friend who dismantled and disposed of questionable things. We stayed put inside the bus for over two hours waiting for Mama's signal. The robbery was all over the news and we watched every story about the incident.

By the third day, Mama had convinced a lawyer friend of hers that we were innocent. He came over to speak with us. Without a weapon, no one could ever convict us of the robbery or the murder, the lawyer explained. What was most incriminating though was the news footage of Ronnie saying he wasn't going down by himself. He was going to take us out with him.

"I have great news for you though," the lawyer informed us. "They have viewed the tape and your friend Ron, or Trouble as you called him, is all over it. Now all you guys have to do is come in with me and let me do the rest."

Tino replied, "Hell, no! I ain't about to walk out of here and go back to jail! I don't believe that one day I'd ever to be free."

NaNa and I agreed with the lawyer, but Bobby never said a word. He got very quiet whenever he was scared.

"I don't know man, something just doesn't feel right to me. Ain't no white man ever tried to help me before," he finally said.

"This is all crazy. We have to start trusting someone," I urged my friends.

"Why now?" asked Tino.

"Because we have run out of options. I am turning myself in. If you never believe anything else that I say, please believe that this is best. Have I ever led you wrong before?"

Tino really shocked me. I thought that he would have been the first to follow, but in the end he was the first to go on his own.

"I love you Pretty Boy but I must go it on my own. I can't go back to jail. The walls were always closing in on me there. I'm afraid to go back. I have to run. I can't say 'yes' to you this time my friend."

Bobby finally said something serious, "Man you can't go it alone, we are a family and we all need each other."

Tino never looked at Bobby, and now it was NaNa's turn to persuade him.

"Big-Dog, as you must admit, and as long as I can remember, you've always been after me. Please take my hand and come with us," she urged.

"No!" he replied defiantly. "I have to go it on my own now. Us following each other has gotten us where we are today. I may have been stupid for all these years, but I ain't no damn fool. I cannot stand the thought of being incarcerated again. All I ever done in my life, really, was listen to you guys. Now I have to go it on my own."

We had never seen Big-Dog cry before, but we could all tell at that very moment he spoke from his heart.

"How come we all couldn't have just been like Blue? Blue was an eagle: led by no one. Now us listening to each other is going to lead us back to jail. No! Hell no! I have to finally be me. I'm gonna be my own man from now on. I'm gonna run so I can finally be free!"

Big-Dog ran out of the door as fast as he could, knowing no one could stop him. He was free for about six hours until the police spotted him crossing an old railroad track on the east side of town. Two cops said they feared for their lives and shot him dead in his tracks. Big-Dog had found his ultimate freedom. He didn't just run out of the bus that night, he ran out of our lives. His ears grew deaf when it was time to listen to his own conscience. At a time when he desperately needed to make a stand, Big-Dog simply turned and ran.

The police viewed the tapes for a couple of hours and we were cleared of all charges. What we had lost in the matter of three and a half days changed us forever.

I married Nana five years later after attending UC Berkeley where we both graduated at the top of our class. The two of us have learned to enjoy life and take it one day at a time. We have two children of our own, and also adopted NaNa's brother and sisters after her mother died.

Bobby went on to become a well-known comedian, and has been on tours all over the world. He's still as funny as ever, and now he's getting paid for it.

John Butler, a.k.a. Blue, is now a hard working businessman in Atlanta and has rental property all over the world. He has three children and a lovely wife. He admitted telling the police who we were, but said it was to save our lives. We never held it against him and Blue never stopped loving us. He just never needed our company to validate who he was. That is a lesson we all had to learn.

We still get together once a year to talk about life and to say a few words about the man we came to know and love as Big-Dog. But more importantly, we talk about how great it is to be an individual.

We must remain mindful of the company we keep and never forget that it is okay to stay behind. There is nothing more debilitating than a man afraid to be persuaded by his own conscience. Fear is a cloud that hovers over the heads of the weak and dismantles their dreams. It devours the shallow souls of those whose spirits aren't deep enough to command more from this world. I was a leader who closed my eyes for a second too long, and led my disciples into a maze of confusion. We were a group of friends without our individual visions. We needed others to fill our superficial voids in our lives. We were afraid to call wrong by its name, so we adopted its premise and were lead by its temptation.

A person's misperceptions or reluctance to acquire knowledge will influence their appetite for fitting in. None of us needs to be led by another. Instead we must believe that we can sustain ourselves through our own journeys.

Our Children Are Watching Us

*S*ince birth, I was taught to hate life and that life hated me. Indirectly I came to believe that God had done something to my skin that caused the white man to believe that he was superior and that his life held more value than mine. What I saw daily crept into my self-consciousness and ate away at my soul. But I know how to speak honestly.

I have never really been in trouble, though I've walked through it in the course of my life. My soul has neither been hugged nor caressed by love. I long to smell the scent of its harmony. Though I bathe my fragile, caramel-coated body daily, I can't seem to wash off the stench of dejection. When asked about my thoughts, I am often slow to speak because it takes me a moment to remove the anger brought on by neglect. My eyes express the sentiments that roam in my heart and dance delicately inside my head.

My hair is long and silky, like fine strings of warm licorice, and its touch has become my safe haven. When all of my chores are done, I sit on the end of the sofa and brush my hair until I fall asleep.

My mama was not big on buying toys or anything like that. I never really had many material things. I was taught to take care of what I had, or else. I learned to amuse myself by putting pretty ribbons in my hair and prancing around like I was special. When no one else was around, I came out of my shell and played the little games that little girls played. I named my only doll Fame and dressed her up real pretty. She was too big to be called Barbie and too short to be a runway model.

Fame was my best friend, my shoulder to cry on, and my pillow to lie on. She recognized me. Her smile set me free. She listened to me as I expressed my dislikes about this world. She was never in a hurry to leave my side. I was too preoccupied with her life to care about my own. Fame was given to me by my grandmother when I was two years old, but she has never aged. She has never changed. She has always been there.

People say that I seem angry because my smiles are hard to come by. You'd have a better chance of catching a falling star than catching a glimpse of a smile upon my face. Maybe my eyes were never meant to touch the beautiful things in life. Maybe I was born to struggle. Maybe I am God's way of punishing my mother.

My mother's name is Angela, but she claimed her nickname was Honey because she was so damn sweet. Ironically she used to call me Satan's daughter until she realized she was indirectly calling herself the devil. But for the better part of my life, she continued to rebuke me in the name of whatever evil was going on inside her head. My anger has been beaten into me by the oppression my mother felt life offered. When children watch the dismantling of a loved one, they will become dismantled as well. I wanted to see the good in life, but it seemed the only way it could ever happen, would be looking at it through somebody else's eyes.

My name is Vicki Patterson, or Button, and there was nothing normal about being Honey Patterson's only child. Nothing at all. I felt like a dirty old washrag. Sometimes she'd clean my skin, but not before washing my soul with the nasty bitterness that surrounded our lives.

Before each sunrise, the rays of hatred would touch my mama's face and penetrate what little empathy she had. She hated the alarm clock almost as much as she seemed to hate me. All hell would break loose as soon as it went off.

"Button! Get your ass up and get ready for school!" she'd yell at me.

My few earthly belongings were kept in the hall closet, always tucked away neatly like Mama wanted them to be. If I didn't put my things away, I knew Mama would beat me. I guess it's okay to say I was brought up rough.

I grew up in the same housing projects my parents lived in as children. In fact, the very same apartment where my grandmother raised Honey was the same one-bedroom, one-bath apartment we lived in. The grass never needed to be cut here in South Dallas because there wasn't any. Trouble originated here and the only thing that grew was the number of niggas. The plumbing creaked and stank, and sometimes the rain leaked into our apartment through the cracks in the ceiling. The whole area was infested with something, if not rodents, it was oppression and neglect.

Dallas was either 'wet or dry.' The expression designated the places you could go and buy liquor. For a long time the only place that you could buy alcohol was in South Dallas, the wet side of town. It wasn't enough that over half of the men in our neighborhood were out of work; they had to establish a liquor store on every corner. There were drugs being sold on every block, or some crackhead was stealing, or a 'ho' was tricking. The sound of madness ringing out through the constant gunshots forever reminded us where we were.

Many of the young boys believed, at an early age, it was easier to just give up at school and sling drugs. Most lacked the presence of a strong figure in their families. There was no one willing to stand up and tell them, that the fiber of our community was being torn down. We lived in a place that had very few rules, yet we had more than our share of self-proclaimed rulers.

Honey was a street hustler, a 'ho,' who slept as hard as she lived. She drank and got high until the sun went down, then she'd throw on barely nothing and took her madness to the streets. I wanted to tell her just how embarrassed I was to see her dress like a 'ho,' but I knew she'd beat me. When she got drunk she became very violent. I was afraid of her beatings, so I stayed away from her as much as I could. The apartment wasn't that big, but I was determined to be wherever she wasn't. She may have loved me in her own way, but very few of her actions displayed it.

She never seemed to feel that she was worth anything, therefore, she became nothing. We were on welfare and Mama thought we were living fairly well. She believed that we had a right to live off of the system. That sounded crazy, but I learned quickly that it wasn't my place to confront her.

I hated looking into her eyes as they became mine and we looked at life through darkness. My soul became infected with the virus of low self-esteem. My moral training ground was built with the props of its foundation. She was the high school beauty queen who allowed the world to steal her crown.

When I was about five years old, I walked through the living room minding my own business. My mother grabbed me and put her cigarette in the middle of my hand.

She shouted, "You little bitch! The next time you see a cigarette butt lying on the floor, ya black ass better pick it up!"

She held the cigarette until it burned a hole in my hand. She shouted, "Do you hear me? Little bitch, do you hear me?"

By way of apology she said, "Button, now you know mother's got a problem..." She paused while lighting another cigarette, then added, "I don't like putting my hands on you child, but you gotta learn to do what I say."

"Okay Mama, I promise I will." Sometimes I felt sorry for my mother. I knew she was never really happy and just took it out on me.

One night before she went out she complained about her hair. I could hear her calling me so I ran into the bathroom.

"Yes, Mama?" I asked, eager to please.

"Girl, bend your head over."

She parted my hair with a comb, and without saying a word, she cut a plug out of the back of my head. As she held up the swatch she said, "Now there, that should be enough. Thanks, Button, now go back in there and play. Mama just needed some bangs."

I was speechless. I ran in my bedroom and cried.

"Girl, you better shut up before I come in there and give you something to cry about."

"Damn girl, that was messed up," I overheard Aunt Nikki tell my mother. "How you gonna just cut that child's hair and glue it on ya head?"

"Bitch, shut up. Glue this shit in, and let's go."

Ever since then I knew that my mama was crazy. They were both crazy. Mama's drinking problem seemed controllable as long as she had some weed to chase it with. Aunt Nikki never seemed to get hers under control. She was a connoisseur of drugs. She did everything there was to do.

Aunt Nikki wasn't really my mother's sister, but one of those women young girls look at and admire from a distance. She was so cool. The things she wore were colorful and cute, and very tight. She had a pretty face, a small waistline and a butt that drove men wild. She had a smile that could brighten up a dark room. She wanted to be a beautician, and at one time she was going to school. But then she got hooked on drugs and she and my mother became the best of friends.

Years ago when Mama hooked up with J.J., Aunt Nikki dated Dermal, my father's brother. Dermal was murdered about five or six years ago and neither J.J. nor Aunt Nikki have ever been the same. She couldn't stand J.J. but they tolerated each other because of my mother. They are still tied by a bond the four of them created one night while drinking and getting high. Aunt Nikki still cries when she thinks about my Uncle Dermal, but the tears are fewer as the years go by.

Aunt Nikki was always hanging out at our place. She'd sleep in the living room, sometimes with me on the sofa, and on the weekends we'd talk through the night about life. Sometimes she would talk to me as if I was her equal. She thought I somehow understood her despite my being so young. She always mentioned how pretty I was and about what she wanted to do with my hair, but she never really told me just how she got her money to support her drug habit. It would destroy her if she found out that I knew. I could tell that the 'dates' she and mama had ate away at her, trick by trick.

She would sometimes take me in her arms and hold me as she cried herself to sleep. She'd say, "Button, I ain't as pretty as you 'thank' I am".

"No Aunt Nikki, you're prettier," I'd reassure her.

She was ashamed of the way she was living, but I loved her despite any shortcomings. She did the one thing my mother never really seemed to have time to do, she held me. She told me, "Hey, Button, your mama is a good person, she just needs to get on her feet, that's all."

I wondered how she was gonna get on her feet by lying on her back?

One day, while Aunt Nikki and Mama laughed and got ready to go out, I got up the nerve to ask Mama why she dressed the way she did.

She answered, "Child, you can't keep honey covered up. Honey needs to breathe. Anyway, how you gonna ask me something like that? I'm yo mama and don't you forget it!"

I knew about Honey's social activities since I was about five or six years old. She turned tricks in the summer, or whenever the weather was decent, over on Montgomery and Bear Streets. It was a well known 'ho' stroll and I was told that, at one time, Honey sold the hottest piece within a twenty-mile radius. It was her claim to fame, but to me it was humiliating.

My father's name is Julian Johnson, but around the town everyone called him J.J. My mother loved his yellowness with a passion. He was a sorry nigga, who slept on his mother's floor until he was thirty-one years old. His mother, my 'ghetto grandmother,' lived directly across from our place. When the weather was bad, Honey brought her johns to the apartment. She would leave a light on whenever a john was inside and my father's job was to be the lookout. He checked the safety signal light to make sure my mother was all right. If the light ever went off he knew to come in a hurry. Not once did the sorry sucker ever think to get me out of there.

They never seemed to care if I was around. They thought I was too young to understand. Those damn fools! Since I learned to walk and talk at an early age you'd think a great big light would have come on in one of their heads.

Something should have told them I was picking up their behavior as well.

Knowing my mother was a 'ho' was painful enough. The fact that my father was pimping her magnified the situation. If that wasn't enough he was also pimping my Aunt Nikki.

I knew the drill though. Mama or Aunt Nikki would wait until a john went into the bathroom then come get me out of bed. I played like I was asleep in case the john happened to come out while Mama placed me on the sofa. Many times, she inadvertently left the bedroom door cracked and I reluctantly watched my mother make money. I learned through watching my mother, how the game was played.

She manipulated men and wrongfully educated my premature mind. She allowed strangers to lay on her, but I couldn't get a toy that had been marked down three times at the corner store. As I grew up the johns became friendly towards me. That was scary and I was ten years old when I had my first sexual encounter. Honey came into our apartment with a john.

His voice blasted across the walls as he went off, "Bitch, I'll kill ya!" he yelled at my mother.

From what I gathered he had fronted her some drug money, and she had gotten too high to perform. When there was a sudden loud noise, I cracked the door just enough to see in the living room. My mother was lying motionless on the floor.

The john put a knife up against her neck. He threatened to kill her if she didn't earn her money, but she was so stoned she didn't hear him.

I ran out of the bathroom crying and begging, "Please stop! Please don't kill my mother! Please, I'll do it."

"Do what?" he asked.

"I know what you want. I've seen my mother do it lots of times. Just don't kill her, please!"

I was so scared, but I had to do it to save Honey's life. I got down on my knees and unzipped his pants. I tried to remember the things I saw my mother do. I thought my mother was squinting at us out of the corner of her eye, and something told me that she wasn't as messed up as she seemed. But soon the man started moaning and I knew I was doing a 'good' job.

When he was satisfied I ran to the bathroom to wash my mouth. Neither Honey nor the john was in the living room when I came back. I looked out the window and saw the two of them laughing like they had pulled off the caper of the century.

It really hurt for my own mother to betray me like that. What kind of drug is so powerful to make a person sell her daughter's childhood, and wipe away her visions of hope? I loved my mother, but sometimes I wished her dead. I hated that I was ever born.

Neither my father nor my mother spoke about what happened that night. But there was one thing for sure, I would never forget it. All I ever really wanted out of life was a decent home environment. They just saw to it that it would never happen. If I had been able to look at a TV that worked more than it was broken, that would have been nice. If I could have had my own bed and not smell every visitor's scent, I could have gotten a decent night's rest. A pair of shoes that wasn't molded by someone else's feet would have done the trick.

I could never understand why my mother chose to let herself go like that. At one time, honey's skin was the color of warm butter. Her body was to die for and her legs were long and luxurious like a runway model. She was as beautiful as any Miss America but she never had the confidence. She gave birth and there wasn't a scar on her body. Big Mama, my grandmother, often said Honey had the body of a goddess and the brains of an ant.

My grandmother was beautiful as well but had been married to a loser, who years ago had run off with her best friend. They seemed to have taken Big Mama's patience and broken her heart. She was never the same, and she couldn't understood how her daughter grew up to become a 'ho' just like her father.

I was welcome at Big Mama's anytime, but my mother had to call before she came by. I could tell that hurt my mother. But like Big Mama often said, it was the choice my mama made. I went by Big Mama's house every day after school to do my homework. She was a retired schoolteacher and made sure that I kept up my grades.

Button is what she called me since as far back as I can remember. When I was a baby I would undo the buttons on everyone's clothes, and if they tried to stop me I would have a fit. To this very day, everybody calls me Button. It's either 'Button' or the 'ho's daughter.' I could tell that Big Mama was ashamed of my mother, but she missed her too. Both of them were too stubborn to give in an inch either way. She wanted me to have better clothes but refused to buy me anything as long as I lived with Honey.

She went to court several times to get custody of me but they never found my mother unfit.

My best friend, in this whole wide world became Zola Anderson. Without her I never would have made it through the fifth grade. Zola was healthy for her age. She was a snacker, with a three-and-a-half-bags-of-chips-a-day habit. She had a way of saying, "Girl, let me tell you…" that made you stop in your tracks and listen to every word. Our mothers' bedroom windows were across from each other and close enough that we could reach out across the buildings and pass notes. Sometimes we'd sit on the windowsills and just talk our heads off like we hadn't seen each other in ages.

Her brother, A.J., had every neighborhood girl's eye, including me. He used to look at me when he thought I wasn't watching. Zola never thought I was interested so she'd tell me about girls who called the house.

One day on my way to school, out of the blue, I felt wetness on my panties. I was so embarrassed. It made me feel cheap and unclean. I told Zola what was happening to me.

She laughed, "Button, what's wrong with you? Don't you know that becoming a woman is a good thing? My period started two or three months ago. Don't worry; I have supplies in my backpack. I'll help you when we get to school."

Zola had an answer for everything. I loved her for being there for me. We both started laughing and hugged each other. I never told my mother about what had happened. I figured it didn't matter to her at all.

Almost a year later Mama complained about missing tampons. Aunt Nikki and I were sitting on the sofa laughing over a joke and I tried to pretend like I didn't hear her. She kept going on and on like someone had stolen her paycheck or her pocketbook.

Finally I answered her, "Yes mama, I took them!"

"Button, why did you mess with my things?"

It finally dawned on her, "Damn, Baby, I'm sorry. When did you get your period?"

"Mama, I got it almost a year ago. Zola told me what to do."

Her only response was, "Oh, that was sweet of her."

My mother was never really a very emotional person, but I could tell she took some pride in my becoming a young lady because she made a point to announce it to all of her friends.

Aunt Nikki started to cry when she heard the news. I couldn't understand what she was carrying on about. I asked her, "Aunt Nikki what's wrong?"

"My little Button is a woman now," she said.

"But why are you crying?"

"Because you ain't my little Button no mo."

I smiled so hard that my face began to hurt. "Aunt Nikki, I will always be your little Button, I promise. Okay?"

I was getting into a lot of trouble by the time I turned eleven. One hot July day I went into the corner store wearing a summer dress but no panties. I had my eyes on a certain store clerk and that day I wanted to show him something. He was about sixteen years old and during the lunch hour he ran the store by himself. Every time I'd go down to the store we'd smile at each other, and on that day I felt like smiling. I was very proud of the length and the texture of my private hair and I wanted to show it off.

When I got there he was busy helping a customer. There was a large fan, which blew real hard, in the corner next to the candy aisle. As soon as the customer left the store, I stepped in front of it and watched the look in his eyes.

"Damn girl, I can see ya!"

"Oh! I'm so sorry! Excuse me, please," I said, while attempting hold my dress down. "Hey, why don't you lock the door and I'll let you see it again."

The boy locked the door as fast as he could.

"What am I going to tell my boss?" he stammered.

"That you had to use the bathroom and didn't want to leave the store unattended."

"Damn, that's smart. How did you think of that so fast?"

"I've been taught to think fast on my feet, but you should see how fast I think on my back," I said with a coy smile. I walked past the fan one more time, and headed to the back room.

"Now if you want to see the rest, get a package of those and follow me."

He grabbed some condoms from behind the counter and ran into the back room with me. "Damn, you're pretty," he complimented me. "Just how old are you?"

"Old enough."

"Damn, I ain't never had nobody before."

"Well today is your lucky day then."

I got down on my knees and did what my mama taught me to do. Then I told him to put the rubber on and lay down on the floor. I had never had sex before but I had seen it done a thousand times. It felt uncomfortable at first but I tried to relax just as I had overheard Aunt Nikki instruct during certain moments. I closed my eyes and moved my hips slowly. He didn't have a lot of strokes in him, but we didn't have much time either. It wasn't long before he finished. I got up and ran out of the store, bleeding ever so slightly, but smiling as he called for me to come back.

I heard him say, "Hey! Come back! What is your name anyway?"

I stopped at the door, turned around for just a moment and said, "Whatever you want it to be!" That's what my mama and Aunt Nikki would tell their johns.

Someone saw me come out of the store and told my grandmother that I had a thing for the store clerk. I was okay with that, just as long as they didn't tell her that I let him place his thing inside me.

Another time I was hanging out on the block with some low-lifes who were up to no good. I was supposed to stay in the house until Mama came home, but there was a loud noise outside, I was bored, and I just wanted to see what was going on. It was late one Saturday and a lot of kids were playing and just being silly.

I overheard that Mookie, a high school dropout, was planning to steal a couple of cars and they needed someone small enough to crawl underneath a fence.

Being the naïve kid that I was, I yelled out, "Hey! I'll do it!"

"You'll do what?" asked Mookie.

"I'll crawl underneath the fence and unlock it for you. I ain't got nothing else to do right now." I just wanted to have some fun that's all. I really wasn't thinking about the consequences. I just wanted to fit in.

"Okay girl. Hell, get ya ass on in," Mookie said. I jumped in the car and went with them.

Mookie had a cute friend who was about two years older than me. I couldn't wait to get next to him. Some of my friends told me that he liked me and I had to admit that I kinda had a thing for him. I didn't know his name; we just called him Little Man or Li-Man for short. I was really hoping that it wasn't because of his size.

"Hey, Button, girl you sure are fine," he said. As I climbed into the back seat next to him he placed his arm around me.

I merely said, "Thank you," and tried to suppress a smile.

It was 1979 and the curl was the 'thang.' Li-Man wore his well. If he had permed his hair, it probably would have been mid-way down his back. On our way Li-man accidentally rubbed his left hand against my breast and said, "Excuse me, Button. I didn't mean to do that."

All I could do was look at him with a silly smile on my face.

There were five of us off to steal a car. Mookie was driving and his sidekick, Big Mike, was a seventeen-year-old eating machine. He smoked weed like it was going to go out of style. He was about six feet tall and was sexy for being so damn fat. There was also Billy, a wanna-be Mack Daddy. He had a nice body, but he had two big teeth that stuck out of his mouth like big elephant tusks. I would have been afraid to kiss him.

When we pulled up to the target area, I jumped out of the car, ran around back, crawled underneath the fence, and came back around to let them in. They were fast. Five minutes hadn't passed and they were on their way out in a new car. My job was done. I was back in the car with Li-Man, who was supposed to drive me home. He threw a tape in the deck and we were on our way back to the projects.

"So what are you gonna do now?" he asked.

"I'm gonna do what you gonna do," I said. It was cold out and my nipples were harder than a Black man's chance at becoming President of the United States of America.

I noticed him staring. "What you looking at boy?" He couldn't answer so I asked, "So what you wanna do? Pull the car over and do what you do," I instructed.

He turned the car into a nearby alley. I let him pull up my blouse and when he unsnapped my bra and my titties stood up like they heard Whitney Houston singing the National Anthem.

I knew that I had beautiful breasts. Mama and Aunt Nikki were always saying, "Girl if we had your breasts we could make a whole lot more money out there on them streets."

As he reached to touch me, I attempted to clarify why everyone called him Li-Man. I unzipped his pants. "Damn, Big-Daddy!" They might have called him Li-Man, but he was 'Big-Daddy' to me.

He asked me to take off my clothes but he didn't have any protection. So I told him I was on my period. I could see the rejection on his face so I worked my mouth on him. He didn't have very good mind control and it wasn't two minutes before it was over.

"Damn girl, that was great! Where in the hell did you learn how to do that?"

I opened the passenger door and spit. I turned and gave him the 'you sure are ignorant look' and told him to take me home. He knew my mother was a 'ho.' He should have just taken his gift and called it a day. No, instead he had to go and mess up the rest of the night.

When we got back to the projects the gang had already repositioned themselves back on the block.

"Where in the hell you been," asked Mookie?

I just got out of the car and went home.

Li-Man said something but I wasn't trying to hear him. I never said another word to him to this day.

Zola was great to be around. She didn't have sex on the brain and she never got into trouble, in school anyway. She didn't clean up her room when she was supposed to, and she was always eating. I could tell that her mother sometimes felt sorry for me. She'd say, "Button why don't you come over and stay with Zola? A.J.'s going over to his father's for the weekend." Most of the time I already knew the invitation was coming, and the few clothes that I had were already packed and ready to go.

Miss Anderson, Zola's mother, was a dark skinned woman who had beautiful teeth and a lovely smile. She had a cute little shape and sometimes when my daddy was at our house he'd take a peak through the blinds. She was a soft-spoken woman who loved her children dearly, but it seemed she loved A.J. more than Zola. She had a problem with Zola's weight and made sure that Zola knew it.

She'd wait for a trouble-free moment then say something like, "Look at Button's waste-line Zola, don't you wish you were built like her?" Zola would smile it off but I could tell the comparisons really hurt.

One day I irritated Miss Anderson when I replied, "Yes my waste line is smaller but she makes better grades than I do."

"Yes, I know her grades are good, but if she didn't eat all the damn time, I could put on a little weight myself." Her disgust with her daughter was apparent.

I loved being over to their apartment. Their place was clean and organized, they had fresh towels, and when they ate dinner, they ate together. Miss Anderson often served fresh vegetables and at my place that kind of thing was foreign. Now and then my mother gave me some money to get me a burger, at a place called Good-Luck's, a couple of blocks over from where we lived.

"Do you and your mother ever go anywhere together?" asked Miss Anderson one day.

"Well, not really," I replied. "I guess you already know that my mother is..."

She interrupted, "No baby don't say that."

"Say what? I was only gonna say that my mother is always sleeping, that's all. What did you think I was gonna say? That my mother is a 'ho?'" I ran to Zola's room to get my things.

Miss Anderson attempted to apologize, "Button, I didn't mean to upset you baby." I acknowledged her with a slight nod.

I knew that my mother was a 'ho.' She certainly wasn't a social worker and the hours she kept eliminated her from being an accountant. But what did that have to do with me? I was fighting to find my own identity at that time and didn't need to be confronted with her activities. She loved the kind of attention men gave her, but she never thought about what kind of attention that would bring me.

Zola and I were walking to school one day when a classmate called me a 'ho.' I tried to act like I didn't hear him, but his voice kept getting louder.

"Hey, 'ho,' how much?" he jeered.

"Just act like you don't hear him, Button," Zola cautioned.

"How do you do that, Zola?" I begged for her help again.

He was a funny looking boy, medium built but short for his age. He had a great big nose that looked like another body part growing out the center of his face. To protect myself, I started to Jones on him.

"Hey! Is that thing growing, or are you just glad to see me? Better than that, why don't you get someone to suck it? They might be able to suck some of those zits off of your face, so that your skin can be soft and smooth like mine. I almost forgot, tell your little daddy that my mother said his check bounced! If he wants some more of her he's gonna have to bring cash from now on."

I will never forget the look on his face. Everyone in ear shot started laughing and from that point on his nickname was 'Dick-Face.' He never called me a 'ho' again and that's all that mattered.

"Button, Button," Zola said trying to get my attention.

"Girl, let me tell you, that was the shit. Damn, where did you learn how to Jones like that? He's probably saying to himself, 'why didn't the bitch just slap me, it would have felt better?' Girl, let me tell you, I'm proud of you. Now do you have any comebacks for fat jokes? 'Cause I sure do need some." Now Zola needed my help.

She smiled as she ate her first bag of potato chips of the day.

I was obsessed with the thought of getting out of the ghetto. I was getting older and needed to leave my mother before her ways started to rub off on me even more. Big-Mama used to say that if you lay down with dirt, you'd get up dirty. I knew there was nothing positive around me. I had nothing to hang on to, and the sounds of my mother and her johns had started to eat away at my soul.

I went to the bathroom once while a john was in the bedroom. I had to pee and just couldn't hold it any longer. The spirit of perversion consumed my thoughts and soon I was masturbating while listening to my mother and the perfect strange in the next room. I had been running from those needs for the better part of my life and now touching myself gave me an outlet that somehow surpassed all my earthly expectations of stimulation. I never looked at my body the same way again. My mother's downtrodden spirit had finally penetrated the moral wall that Big-Mama had built for me.

I never thought touching myself would give me so much pleasure, and the next morning I got up on my own, just like I had done for the better part of my life, but this time with a smile upon my face.

I was smart for my age and just as pretty as my mother. I dressed in a tight shirt a pair of my mother's old jeans. They fit me perfectly. I went next door to meet Zola before we went to school and watched the expression on her face.

When she first saw me she exclaimed, "Damn, who dressed you this morning? Your Aunt Nikki?"

"It's my knew look, do you like it?" I replied.

"Yes, I guess," she said slowly. "It's gonna take a little getting used to though."

I could tell that Zola wasn't comfortable with the lie she just told, but I appreciated her not wanting to hurt my feelings.

Later that day while everyone was at lunch I crept into the girls' bathroom and masturbated for the second time in my life. It felt like I was a kid who had found a new toy. I felt like something was wrong with me but I was all right with the experience. My biggest test would be when I went to do my homework at Big-Mama's house.

She was usually resting when I got there. I had my own key and let myself in as usual. In the kitchen I poured myself a drink. My back was turned when Big-Mama when she came in. She was singing an old spiritual but stopped suddenly.

"Honey!" she shouted at the top of her lungs. "You know you need to call before you come by my house!"

I turned around slowly. "Big-Mama, it's me Button," I said meekly.

I was getting ready to look for her glasses so she could see me clearly, but I noticed she already had them on.

She just stared at the image that looked like her daughter while realizing that it was me, her only grandchild. It immediately caused her heart to become sad. Her spirit reached my soul and I could tell she was hurting.

"Baby, what happened to your face? And why in the hell are you wearing those jeans?"

"Big-Mama, I found them in the back of Honey's closet," I explained. What's wrong with them?"

"Child, those are the jeans your mother was wearing the first time I caught her walking on Montgomery and Bear. Child, those jeans are too tight for you to have on. Please don't ever wear them again. There is something evil about this way of dressing."

"Oh Big-Mama, ain't nothing gonna happen to me. I can handle these clothes."

"All right, Button. You listen to me. That's what your mother said years ago. Now look at her, she still stuck on stupid."

After finishing my homework, I gathered my things and went home. By the time I got home Big-Mama had already called Honey and cursed her out. She must have really upset my mother because she was awake, just setting there in the living room with tears in her eyes. I thought she was engulfed in sadness and realization.

She was not willing to take full responsibility for her actions though. She said, "How could you embarrass me like this, Button? What in the hell were you thinking about? Take my damn clothes off and don't you ever let me see you dressing like that again!"

A sense of urgency suddenly came over me and I bravely began to speak. "Mama what's with you? What is wrong with the clothes I have on?"

"They're mine, that's what's wrong!" was all she could admit.

I knew she wasn't gonna buy me the type of clothes that I wanted to wear, so I told her I wanted a job.

"Who's gonna hire you?" she scoffed. "You can't do nothing but set around the house and eat. Go ahead and try to get a job. You'll see, ain't nobody hiring us."

I couldn't believe my mother had so little faith in me, but at least I had become immune to her cutting words. That's the way it was, she always spoke and I was supposed to listen. My views didn't matter so I rarely ever spoke. Before I could ask her what Big-Mama had said, she had fallen back to sleep.

I was confused and in need of some emotional healing. My mind was telling me I was going to be all right, but I needed to hear that from someone I loved. Aunt Nikki was always too damn stoned to feel herself, much less feel for my needs. It was Friday and Zola was going to her father's for the weekend. I had no one to talk to. I even searched for Fame but was afraid Mama had thrown her out years ago.

That day I went downtown to fill out some job applications, but no one was hiring. I had my hair fixed and did the best I could with the clothes that I had. People were trying to talk to me, possibly thinking I was older. Suddenly it hit me. Nobody knew how old I was and I didn't have to tell them. I needed money and I didn't know but one way to make it. I thought about doing something simple for ten or twenty dollars. I could do it for a little while and then just quit.

As I was getting off of the bus, a well-groomed gentleman walked up to me and said, "Hey pretty lady, you look familiar. Have I ever seen you anywhere?"
"No, I don't think so," I assured him.
"Are you old enough for me to buy you a drink?" he asked.
I replied with a simple question, like Aunt Nikki had said hundreds of times, "Mr. what is it you want with me?"
"Well I just wanted to show you a good time," he offered.
"Well, let's see. What is your interpretation of a good time?"
"I'm not going to have sex with you, if that's what you're getting at. But if you want to show me a good time, I'm willing to take a shot at it. My car is over there," and he pointed at a Mercedes Benz sedan across the street. I thought he had to be somebody big because his car was so big. I'd seen movie stars on TV drive the same six-class.
"Let me see your driver's license."
"Why do you want to see my license? Are you some kind of cop?"
"No, but I've been taught to protect myself, and I don't have a lot of time to waste." I looked at his ID and said, "So let's go."
"Are you sure that you've never done this before?" he asked skeptically.
"No," I lied. "Let's just say that I've been around it all of my life. Now when we get in the car, pull your pants

down to your knees, turn the radio on, and I'll do the rest." I tried to remember things my mother would say to her to johns.

"Okay, but how much is it going to cost me?"

"Well, I charge thirty dollars to start, but that will be up to you when I get through."

I spit out my gum, entered the passenger's door and braced myself as I begin to suck my first john. I could feel his head swelling inside my mouth as I stroked the tip against my warm lips. I knew what I was doing. I had been taught by the best, Honey and Aunt Nikki.

"Okay now," I said as I took a break. "To start was thirty dollars, what is it worth for me to finish?"

He looked down at me and offered forty.

I looked up into his eyes and said sweetly, "Now come on. You can do better than that." He fought to keep his composure, as I was getting ready to complete Aunt Nikki's instructions. She'd always say, suck him dry, or until he cries, whichever comes first.

I stopped suddenly as if I had heard a sound. He said, "What in the hell are you stopping for?"

"Didn't you hear that? I thought I heard a noise," I said to continue my ploy. "Do you want me to finish?"

"Hell ya, I want you to finish."

"Okay, then. Get me some more money."

"What do you mean more money?"

"Mr., did I stick to my deal and suck you completely? Did I do it right?"

"Yeah, sure."

"Well, it's not my fault that you didn't come. Let's go and get some more money and I might let you play with me just to make things even."

I began stroking again, this time as fast as I possibly could. "Hey Mr., do you have an ATM card?"

"What kind of person are you?" he chortled.

"Well, I'm the kind of person you pay to play."

The man continued to smile as I continued to stroke, and we were on our way to the bank.

When he returned to the car he said eagerly, "Okay, I've got money. Let's finish what we started. I know a place where we can go."

We turned down a street and we went into a different bank that he claimed to own. Upstairs we entered an office that he said was his. A part of me felt that I had hit the jackpot and I knew what to do. I had been indirectly groomed to star in this role. He cleared off the top of his desk and I laid him down on his back. I began to suck the gold out of his rich dick. I stroked his nuts like Tiger Woods stroked his putter when the game is out of hand.

"Now you told me that you were going to let me play with you," he said.

My rates had risen. 'Twenty for the outside, fifty to get inside. Hands only." He was willing to pay and reached for my purse.

I knew that he would see I had a gun so I held out my hand and took another seventy dollars. I placed the money inside my purse and I placed his hands inside my panties. I could tell he was pleased by the way he trembled and moaned. And of course the three hundred dollars really showed me that he was pleased. Within an hour and a half I had made more money than both Aunt Nikki and Honey had in a month.

I had pulled off my first trick, and the rich john said he was going to set me up with his friends in the coming weeks. He dropped me off down town and we made plans to meet again the next week.

On my way back home I stopped and bought some sexy clothes. I even bought some make up and nice earrings. I wasn't in a hurry to get home because there was no one there to talk to. I knew Big-Mama wouldn't be proud of me for what I had done. It bothered me to think of what she'd say if she knew I was following in my mother's footsteps.

In the coming weeks I had many dates and turned many tricks. The thought of making that kind of money so fast gave me a high like I had never known. Lance, my Mercedes john, hooked me up with all his friends like he promised. All of my them were Caucasian and each one of them was well off. Two of them wanted to move me over to the north side of town. None of them knew that I was only fifteen, and some had children older than me.

I especially enjoyed being with them, first because they weren't cheap, and second I just never thought that I could ever charge my brothers like I charged the white man. They liked me because I was young and had very little miles. I took pictures of them because Aunt Nikki told me that I should always try to protect myself.

I stayed in shape and learned to groom my body like rich ladies in fashion magazines. I lost weight so that I could fit the mold and I even started getting Aunt Nikki to do my hair. She could finally say she was a beautician.

"Girl," she would say, "you really do have a very nice boyfriend to be spending all this kind of money on you. All I can say is be safe and remember not to come home with no babies."

I paid her top dollar, insisting that my boyfriend told me to make sure my hairdresser was given a good tip.

Mama said, "Child if J.J. would have ever bought me that kind of shit, I wouldn't have to sell nothing."

She didn't know that I was capitalizing on the same 'nothing' she was practically giving away. I was Button by day and became 'Precious' by night. I began living a double life and my grades were falling fast.

I couldn't stay awake at school and the teachers started calling home to inquire about the change in my behavior. I had been an A and B student and they knew that something was wrong. Many times, my mother was too high to answer their questions. She began to curse them out if they called while she was sleeping. They sent a social worker out to see what was going on. They even contacted my grandmother but she wasn't willing to respond as my legal guardian. I suppose her spirit told her I was in the midst of evil doings and she just didn't want to have anything to do with me anymore.

I didn't see Big-Mama for a long time after that. Neither one of us wanted to face facts. I wanted to continue being 'Button' but this 'thang' had me going. I was out of control and sex was the only 'thang' on my mind. Besides I loved the thought of getting paid.

I learned how to ride with a rhythm that made me more money. I was freakier than my mother and my back was stronger. I was better than she was, because I worked while

I was sober, with my eyes always open. It cost my johns fifty dollars just to look, and two hundred more to touch.

J.J., Honey and Aunt Nikki got hooked on crack, the new drug going around. I was supporting their habit by making two and three hundred dollars a shot. I made over a thousand dollars a week and I only worked when I wanted to. Some of my dates lasted only fifteen to thirty minutes. Sometimes I didn't even have sex. I was taken on numerous shopping sprees all because I was able to please a man in bed.

Having a mother who was a 'ho' was a reality I fought with constantly. I knew the things that were happening to me were the result of how I was finally coping with it. I never thought that my life would lead me to this, and through the darkness I hoped the sun had not stopped shining on me. One day I planned to be able to go to college and do something good with my life. For now I was a 'ho,' who masked the evil by labeling herself a 'call girl.' Whether I got a call or not, I was a 'ho' all the same.

For the most part I missed out on the hugs and kisses in life. I hated that things hadn't turned out better to that point, but I was alive even if my soul was crying. I knew that I'd be all right even if death came calling. I had an answer for it though. I was more afraid to continue living in a world filled with pain than I was of dying while attempting to relieve myself of its pressure.

A year and a half passed before I knew it. I did manage to graduate from high school. Everyone came but Big-Mama. Even though my age was finally exposed, one john bought me a car for my graduation gift. He paid for me to park it downtown.

I began to date more frequently and moved over on the north side of town. I had made a personal plan and began to put it into action. First, I needed to talk to someone I could trust and called on Zola. She was attending a local junior college and still lived with her mother.

When she first heard my voice, she sounded happy to hear from me. "Hey girl what's going on? Why did it take you so long to call? You know, don't nobody know how to get in touch with ya," she laughed.

"I've been working things out," was all I could say. Zola knew I was always lying about where I was going and about the things I was doing. "Did you get that money I left with your mother?" I asked.

"Sure, Button. You know my Mama couldn't wait to give it to me, so that she could ask me how you got it."

"I think it's a good thing what you're doing - taking care of your mother and all, but she's not looking very good lately," I said.

"Yeah girl, I know. She's lost a whole lot of weight. Her pants can't even stay up," she lamented.

"What else can I do to help, Zola?"

"Shit, Button, just keep on trying I guess." I could tell she shrugged off my offer to help. "What's up with ya sorry daddy?" she asked, changing the subject.

"I don't know. Why do you ask?"

"Well, you know that TV set you bought your mama about a month ago?"

"Yeah, what about it?"

"Are you sitting down?"

"Why? Why do I need to be sitting down?"

"Well I could be wrong, but two nights ago, I could have sworn that I saw him carrying it out of your mother's house."

"Hell no! Hell no! Girl, let me get up off this phone and call over there."

"Well that's going to be even harder to do."

"Damn, why you say that?" She was making me ask too many questions.

"Well, my mother said just today she saw your daddy selling a phone to a man at the liquor store."

I was so mad but just laughed out loud and said, "Well it's a good thing that I have you go and pay her rent for me. If it wasn't for you, she'd be homeless by now."

The phone was quiet but I could hear Zola breathing on the other end. She was trying her hardest not to let me know that she was crying.

I said, "Zola what's wrong?"

"I just don't want you to end up like your mother."

"No, no, Zola. It won't ever happen to me. I put that on everything I love. I have a plan that I feel will work. I just need you to help me pull it off."

Zola had always been good with numbers in school and I was going to need someone who could help me handle a lot of money. There was a major political convention coming to town and twenty of the top call girls in Dallas were placed on a special list. My name was already on it.

Many of my clients, congressmen, senators, and countless others would be attending the convention. When I started having sex with most of them I was only fifteen years old. They would be ruined if their names were to be mentioned with mine. If my plan worked, by

Monday evening I would be on a plane headed towards economic freedom. Over the years I had compiled numerous photographs, tapes and videos for this very moment.

"Zola, what are you doing this Friday?"

"Uh, nothing," she said hesitantly.

"Well don't plan anything. I m gonna need your help to get out of this game." I could tell Zola was smiling. I asked, "Are you with me?"

There was a pause before she said five big beautiful words, "Girl let me tell ya..."

"Then it's a date!" I exclaimed.

"You better know it," she was quick to agree.

It was Wednesday evening when I phoned Zola next.

"Okay girl, here goes the plan. I'm gonna need a couple of your drama classmates to pull this off," I started.

"Girl, let me tell ya, this sounds like something I've always wanted to do."

Zola always wanted to be in the movies and this was her chance to feel like a star. In fact, she was more excited than I was.

"Girl, I know just the right people for this job." She was hooked. "You're gonna love me for this."

"Okay, okay," I said with great anticipation. "Get them together and come to my new apartment at seven o'clock on Friday night, okay?"

"Sure," Zola said. "We'll all be there."

I had already developed my film and had three copies of everything piece of incriminating evidence. The day had finally come for me to get out of the game. When

Zola arrived at my place with her group of people I was surprised to see her mother with her.

I was overwhelmed when she said, "Look Button, this is my chance to make things right for hurting your feelings years ago."

Zola said, "Button, you never knew this but my mother won best drama student in high school. This has gotta be something she can do for you."

A.J. was with them as well. He interjected, "I wasn't going to miss out on this, Button. After all, who do you think had to listen to them rehearse for this, the role of their lives, all these years?" I was tearing up.

"Okay, Zola, now who is this?" I sniffled.

"Oh, this is Bony, one of the best damn con-artists I know. I thought you'd need one of them to pull this off. Hell, he's so good he cons me out of my chips." We all started laughing and walked into the living room.

"Damn, Button, are you rich?" asked A.J. as he surveyed the place.

"No, not hardly, but I will be when this is over. Here's the plan," I said and started to explain." I guess by now everyone here knows what I do for a living."

"No, show us," Bony replied with a big smile.

"Okay, now, let's get serious. I'm a call-girl," I admitted, "and have been one for a little over three years. Here on these tapes and in these pictures is enough evidence to make me rich and get out of the game for good."

Miss Anderson moved to the edge of the couch. "What do you want us to do?" she asked.

"Well, since you're here," I addressed her directly, "you're gonna be my mother."

"A.J., you're gonna be my jealous boyfriend who just happened to have found these pictures and tapes."

"Damn, that's cool," Bony said. "I saw a movie like this a long time ago." I could tell he didn't want to be left out.

"Okay, Bony it's your turn. You have to be a minister asking for a ransom."

"Ransom?" he asked innocently.

Zola popped him in the back of the head, "Ya dummy! Ransom - that's when you tell someone that you have something they want. They want it so bad, they'll exchange a lot of money for it."

"Now be quiet," I said to everyone. "Okay, I need you guys to come with me. I have a friend who owns a costume store down the street, and he is waiting for us."

A.J. said, "Cool, we get to dress up and everything."

I smiled at him. I hadn't seen him in a long time, but he was still fine.

After we were fitted for our perspective roles, we rushed back to my place to film the ransom tape. Bony, he missed his calling. He was so good as the pleading minister I almost started clapping.

Miss Anderson played my mother. Zola was right; her mother was a drama queen. She was so convincing that for a minute I almost thought that she was Honey. She was begging the prospective listeners to help identify everyone on the tape and bring them to justice. She made it look like all my troubles were the johns' fault, and I loved her for the emotion she put into her role.

Zola played my lawyer. When she was made up and in her wig she looked just like Jacquelyn Mosley, a prominent Texas attorney. Ms. Mosley hadn't lost a case in ten years and there wasn't one attorney in Texas eager to go up against her.

On the tape we were seen leaving my apartment together, as she gave me a big hug and handed me her business card. Bony brought it all home claiming to have counseled me in my lowest hour. He went on and on about children being abused on our streets and how the individuals on this tape needed to be brought to justice. He was good. He made me want to go back to church.

"There will not be any more practice runs," I cautioned the group after a few hours. "I've gone over my plan with you all four or five times now. At ten o'clock the real show will begin." They all left to take their places.

I had asked Lance Hanson to show up at my place at ten. He was fingered as the ringleader. He had been the one who introduced me to all the others, and if we could take him down, all the rest of the johns will fall with him.

I placed our homemade ransom tape in the VCR and set the universal remote on the table. Miss Anderson and Zola sat in a car across the street and listened in on everything via two-way radio. It wasn't long before Lance showed up.

I was sitting on the sofa, sipping chardonnay when the doorbell rang. I was wearing screaming heels and a long, see-through peignoir. I said in my deepest, most sexy voice, "Come in, Lance."

He opened the door with flowers in his hand. I walked over to kiss him and accepted the flowers.

"Don't just stand there, Lance, have a seat. Can I pour you a glass of wine?"

His blue eyes were caressing my body head to toe. I moved slowly, excited to be turning him on. I put the flowers in a vase, took his coat, and handed him a glass of wine. He was embarrassed by his inability to sit at the moment.

I said, "Now Lance, are you happy to see me or what?"

Through a previous background check I knew Lance was indeed a millionaire, but he had been arrested once for taking pictures of children. He obviously wouldn't want the public to know that he had been dating me since I was only fifteen.

I got down on my knees and started attending to his discomfort. While he was moaning, I turned on the TV. Shortly Lance's prided johnson became short.

"What's wrong?" I asked innocently.

He pushed me away and shouted, "What in the hell is going on, Precious? What are you doing to me?"

A.J. was a tall muscular, twenty-one year old black brother. To most white people that was intimidating. Lance seemed to be no exception. A.J. knew his cue, and there was a sudden loud knock on the door. It wasn't locked because I needed Lance to be caught with his pants down.

"What in the hell is going on? Bitch, who is this?" A.J. demanded as he stormed into the apartment.

I pretended to be afraid. "This is Lance, my boyfriend," I blurted out.

"No! Hell no! I'm not her boyfriend," he said defensively.

A.J. looked at Lance closely and said, "That's the bad ass white boy I saw on that tape!" he yelled.

"There's got to be something I can do to make this right," Lance begged. He knew his sudden predicament.

A.J. went off by saying, "Hell yeah, you son-of-a-bitch, there is something you can do." He went over to the VCR and pulled out the tape. He pulled a gun out of his pocket and placed it to the side of Lance's head. He whispered softly in his ear, "I know who you are now. You're that perverted millionaire who took pictures of those children a few years back."

Then he looked over at me and asked, "Bitch, how long has this been going on?"

I thought of everything I could that made me feel sad. It was enough to create real tears. "For over three years," I sobbed out a confession.

A.J. looked back at Lance and accused, "You mean that you've been having sex with her since she was fifteen?"

Lance fell to his knees with his face in his hands. "Please," he begged. "I did not know that she was underage."

"Well, now you do," said A.J. " So no this is what you're gonna have to do," he instructed as he outlined my plan for Lance. "I want you to call every single person on this tape. You tell them that if they don't each place one million dollars in this account by three o'clock on Monday, I will be taking this tape to Ms. Mosley."

"A million dollars a piece? You've got to be out of your mind!" Lance exploded.

"Yessir," A.J. agreed. "That's what they all say. Here, take this tape with you so your buddies will know what they're paying for. By the way, the first million dollars is for the first two tapes only. The third tape and these photos will remain in a safe deposit box. The police will be shown if something should ever happen to Button".

"Button? Who's Button"?

"I meant Precious of course. Just do as I say and have the money deposited by three o'clock on Monday."

A.J. grabbed Lance's coat and said, "Look. Zip your pants up and get the hell out of here! As soon as Lance left, Zola, Bony and Miss Anderson came back into the apartment.

"Girl, you were something else," Zola said.

By the time they had arrived I had covered myself with my robe. A.J. said, "Damn, if you think that's something, you should have seen her a couple of minutes ago."

I smiled at A.J. saying, "Shut up boy! Y'all, should have seen A.J. He was a damn fool!"

"Hey, let's all go over to my place and celebrate," said Miss Anderson.

I changed my clothes and we all headed towards the projects. We made a stop by the corner liquor store and I treated everyone to his or her bottle of choice. We even went by 'Good-Luck's' to get burgers and link baskets. I wanted to have a big party to celebrate my coming out. Things had gone according to plan and I felt that everything would turn out for the better. I just wanted to get out of the ghetto, and I wanted all my loved ones to get out as well.

I never wanted to be like my mother. Life had put me on a merry-go-round but now I refused to ride it for the duration. At eighteen, I was still young enough to start over. There was a time I felt I had no way out, but God always seemed to have the final word. I refused to give my soul to the devil, so I prayed everyday to be shown the spirit of Job. I wanted the world to forgive me for all of my transgressions. I just wanted to be happy.

I knew I couldn't stay in the game any longer without feeling its full effects, so I listened to the pleas of my friends. Zola and I started planning for the day that we could get out as winners. When we went into Zola's apartment, it was all I could do not to visit my mother. I knew she was hurting, but I resisted my craving to attend to their needs. Neither my mama nor my daddy had ever done anything to preserve my well-being. I never seemed to matter to them at all. Why did I still want their love?

We lifted up our glasses, toasted to life and prosperity, but we never forgot that our roots were firmly planted in oppression. We smiled contentedly, but never relinquished our reality. I was relieved by the fact that my mind had not become irreversibly tainted. The lustful thoughts of man had afflicted my mother and caused her heart to cave. If I could listen to the voices that spoke endlessly to my soul, I could find the answers. By stopping the cycle of madness, I could step away.

I created an opportunity to start a new life for myself. I had to relocate so that my man-to-be would never have to feel the spirit of my past. In time I would have to tell him of the roads on which I had traveled. I knew that whoever he might be, one of his greatest traits would have to be self-confidence.

Monday evening came and went, and shockingly I had twenty million dollars in the bank. I had made a new life for myself, and pledged to do right by those who did right by me.

I took care of the women in my family. Me and Big-Mama made up and are the best of friends. She's never asked for much, but I make sure she has a nice monthly income. I placed both my mother and Aunt Nikki into an exclusive drug-rehab program and they kicked their habits. I bought Aunt Nikki a hair salon over on the north side of town and she is the hottest thing going. I bought my mother a home as well and furnished it in all of the colors she loves. Her skin is back to its original honey color and she's never been more beautiful than she is today.

I still have a hard time convincing her that she did all of those crazy things to me. She doesn't remember putting a cigarette out in my hand, or taking a plug out of my hair to make those bangs she wanted, or when she and my no-good father set me with a john. I guess it's best that we put all those crazy things behind us.

I bought each of my friends a house and a car and took them out of the hood. I paid for Zola's tuition and attended college myself. I received a degree in business and three years later earned a master's in the same field.

Today Zola and I are partners in several business ventures. We learned how to buy low and sell high and became financially independent. We are both happily married to wonderful men, and the four of us take annual vacations together.

As parents and guardians of our youth we must be more selective about the company we keep. Many of us don't realize just how much influence we have over our children. Directly or indirectly, our actions do affect them, and the consequences can be devastating. Luckily the consequences of my thoughtless actions were not irreversible.

We must remain mindful of the way we are perceived in the eyes of those not yet strong enough to make their own way. What we do today will many times reflect what our offspring shall be tomorrow. It is through our eyes that they can be shown their future. Take care to remember, "our children are watching us."

Nicoli Is My Name

I was born on the eve of trouble and ten months later learned to walk before the sun went down on the west side of danger. Even though love was only a step away, I chose to run with a fearless group of my peers. Living on the edge of emotional corruption was more exciting than being hugged by a loved one. I chose to remain closer to the sunset of transgression. Its pull was stronger and hatred was more plentiful and readily available than any feeling of love.

Our eyes were fixated on the negative things of this world. While staring at what we called reality, I became engulfed by its lies and allowed hatred to become my friend. Though I craved patience my mind refused to caress its presence. Its touch was fleeting and I didn't experience it for any extensive period of time. I realized, though, how truly precious life is. I became a man while walking down the misguided streets of self-inflicted oppression.

My mother's name is Samone Renee Jackson, but those who know and love her simply call her Sam. She is the strongest person I know and the glue that holds us all together. She is stronger than black coffee. She is self-reliant, and at times as bullheaded as they come. When faced with a challenge, she never hesitates to take it head on. She is in her mid-thirties and has never had a problem speaking her mind. If needed, she is as direct as all ten of the commandments. We check our attitudes at the front door before entering the Jackson household.

I have seen her overcome great odds, watching as she navigated us through some very rough times. She has never craved the strength of a man nor has she cried out for his leadership. She has worked as a private duty nurse for as long as I can remember, and demands that her house is always clean.

My mother is the product of an interracial couple; my grandmother is Caucasian and my grandfather is Black. My mother inherited her mother's fair skin. I have three older sisters who, along with my mother I proudly call my 'Four Queens.' Since birth they have always looked out for my best interests and have tried their best to mold me into a strong, productive individual. Nicoli is my name.

I have a stepfather named Jimmy McCullen, who is a manager at the local energy plant in town. He seems to be very important. People call on him for answers to all kinds of questions. To his credit he never treated me any different than his daughters, and they never mixed words about whose father he is. He is my sisters' father. But my three older sisters, Taylor, Lauren and Rae, along with my mother, I call my 'Four Queens.'

Taylor, for whatever reason, has never really paid me very much attention. That is until I get on her nerves. There is something about her room that makes me want to go in unannounced. I know it's her biggest pet peeve. She's tried everything that she can to keep me out but, still, I find my way back in.

Lauren is into her own thing. She's a reader and a thinker. We don't really get along that well either. She calls me stupid and crazy all the time, like she was qualified to do so. We could never be left alone for any period of time. She was only eight years old when she already labeled me her worst enemy. Sometimes I'd wander around in her room just to get the friction going. The way she yelled out for my mother did something to me. Making her angry gave me a great emotional high.

Rae and I were the best of friends. I loved her gentle heart. She always felt she had to protect me. Sometimes she would catch me making fun of one of my other sisters and say, "Nic, leave them alone and sit down." She had a quiet way of settling me when the world was frustrating. I never pretended not to notice her love.

Jimmy and my mother used to mess around years ago, long before I was conceived. My mother wouldn't ever marry him because she felt that every man she met was trying to get the family home. She swore that no man would ever get his hands on it as long as she lived. Consequently, Mr. Jimmy was never allowed to stay over for more than three days at a time, and my mother never bent that rule. She had his girls and washed his clothes but she wasn't about to give him the deed to the house.

She had me while Mr. Jimmy was away fighting for our country. While Mr. Jimmy was risking his life, my mother met Malik, my father. Sometimes it seemed that my sisters resented me for what my mother did behind their father's back.

There were times after he had come home from the war, my mother would turn to him and say, "Now Jimmy, that's what you get. Don't look at me. I told your ass not to leave." Mama had him whupped, as the old folks would say.

Sometimes he would come over to watch us when she went out on the town with her friends. He was better at cooking than he was at being a man. He had a heart that was too kind and a backbone that was hard to find. The way my mother treated him was wrong. But who could really blame her? He loved her unconditionally and never seemed to mind her insulting comments. I could tell that he embarrassed his daughters by having neither the strength nor the courage to speak up for himself.

One night my mother made him go home in his underwear. They had gone to bed but he hadn't taken a bath. No sooner had he climbed under the covers than she started in on him.

"Get your ass up Jimmy! Haven't I told you that you couldn't sleep in my bed without taking a bath?"

"Hey, Sam. Not so loud," he quietly replied. "The children are going to hear you."

"I don't care. They need to know it's wrong for a man to come to bed smelling like this."

She walked over to his side of the bed and picked up his pants. She took his car keys out of the pocket, but threw all his clothes out of the window into a dumpster.

"Now get your stanky ass out of my house!" she yelled. My mother had been drinking and the liquor had gotten to her.

By that time I was out of my bed and had started up the stairs to check out all of the commotion. Mr. Jimmy was walking down the hallway towards me, keys in hand. He was wearing a pair of underwear that appeared small enough to fit me. I had never seen a more hurt and shameful man. He was too weak to fight and too hurt to cry.

The three girls stood in the hallway. Rae walked over to her father and gave him a small blanket. My oldest sister, Taylor, ran to my mother's bedroom door and shouted, "How could you embarrass him that way, Mama? He's a man, not a dog! What are our neighbors going to say?"

"Let them say whatever they want to say. They know his ass is weak."

"You could have at least given him back his clothes," Rae said as she walked back to her room.

Needless to say, Mr. Jimmy and my mother were never the same again. It was hard for him to face us and he stayed away for a long time. That was until the 'evil spirit' came calling.

Mr. Jimmy had been smoking since high school. After seeing doctors for over five months, he was diagnosed with lung cancer in its latter stages. There was nothing to do but to prepare for the worst. Within six months Mr. Jimmy passed on. Before he left, he told my sisters to not to hate their mother for anything that had taken place.

My mother took his passing worse than anyone else. As they lowered his body into the ground, she kept saying, "Jimmy, please forgive me. I'm so sorry."

Lauren held her father's death against my mother the longest. She felt that he could have fought the cancer if only Mama had loved her father the way he needed to be loved.

"You took my father from me!" she yelled out at my mother while we were still at the gravesite. "What did he ever do to you, Mother, but try to love you? Now look at what you've done. Look at you. Look at us. You've killed the only man that ever really cared about you."

My mother never responded to Lauren. Maybe a part of her felt Lauren was justified. Or maybe she was just grieving too hard to find the strength to lash back. Anyway, we all got past it, and that's all that really matters.

My mother has never taken a drink since Mr. Jimmy's passing. She re-committed her life to the Lord and asked for forgiveness.

One sad Sunday when I was no more than six years old, we had just come from church. I remember Mama coming into my room. She sat down on the foot of my bed and said, "Nic, I want to tell you something."

"What's that, Mama?" I asked.

"Well, you've been asking about your dad for a while now and it's time that you hear the truth. Nic, your father passed away while I was carrying you."

"What does that mean, Mama? Carrying me?"

We had gone to church early that morning and the schoolteacher had been teaching us about death. The sermon was about death as well, and that inspired my mother to talk to me.

"Nic, do you know where your father is?"

"Yes, Mama. He's gone to heaven to visit Jesus."

"Yes, Baby, that's right."

"Why did you ask me Mother? Did you forget where Malik was?"

She was surprised I remembered his name. "No, I am just trying to make sure that you know."

"Yes, Mama, I know where he is. Well, I miss him. Do you ever miss him?"

"Yes, as a matter of fact sometimes I do. Sometimes Baby, I see him in my dreams. He was a fine man. Built strong, just like you."

I remember smiling hard enough to light up the room, but she broke down in tears.

"What's wrong, Mama? Did I say something that made you sad?"

"No child, you could never say anything to make me feel sad."

"I was just thinking about how much I miss your father. That's all."

"Mama, do you have any pictures of my daddy?"

"No, Baby. Your father was funny. He never liked to take pictures, but I want you to know if you ever have any questions about him, please come and ask me." But after seeing my mother break down and cry as we reminisced, I didn't want her to feel bad anymore, so I refused to talk about him.

For nearly two more years I never mentioned his name. I had come to grips with the idea of never having a father.

Though the wondering never ceased, my questions did. I was determined to sacrifice my feelings for my mother's, but if I did hear his name, my eyes flew wide open and my ears were at attention.

One day, on the way home from school, Mama and I stopped at a local grocery store not far from the house. She had to pay some bills. Out of nowhere I heard someone say the name Malik. I was holding my mother's hand and before she knew it, I pulled my hand free. I tried to follow the voice to the other side of the store.

"Where do you think you're going?" she called after me.

Apparently she hadn't heard the man yelling out Malik's name. I was prepared to receive a beat-down for a glimpse at a man who might have fathered me.

"Nicoli, if you don't come back here right now, I'm gon beat your ass!" I heard Mama yell.

"I'll be right back, Mama! I think I saw a friend from school," I lied as I made my way through the store. I knew I had disobeyed and I could hear her threatening me under her breath. I continued, though, and turned a corner in the store, headed towards the voice I had heard.

By that time my mother was first in line to pay her bills. She had a decision to make: either run and catch me or stay put and do what she had come to do. She just stood there, angry with me for running off.

There I was running around the store, hoping that I could at least find the man who called out my father's name. Was I attempting to find a person who was never lost? Was I looking for the face of a father I had never seen? No sooner had I reached out to touch the back of the man's coat, when I experienced a hot flash of fire running down my back. It was Mama's famous backhand. She had struck me firmly on the left side of my neck and stopped me dead in my tracks.

"Child, haven't I told you to never speak to strangers?"

"Yes Ma'am. But I thought that he was my father."

She looked confused and placed one of her hands on her hip. "Child, what made you think that he was your father?"

"Well…"

"Well, what? Speak up, Nicoli."

"Well, I heard a man call out the name Malik, and I thought…"

Before I could finish she grabbed both of my cheeks. "No, Nicoli. Don't think right now. Child, let me think for you. Just because you hear the name Malik doesn't mean the man is your father! That man is not your father. He is the wrong height, the wrong build, and your father wouldn't ever wear a coat like that!

"Nicoli, there are some crazy people in this world, just waiting on a chance to do mean things to little boys like you. So please promise that you'll never run off again."

"Mama, I will never do it again, I promise." I never got a chance to touch the man's coat, nor did I ever see his face. All I remember was Mama grabbing my arm and leading me towards the door. There were times when my feet were barely touching the floor. As people watched, a great big smile grew on her face. It didn't take a genius to see that it was fake. I could tell she was mad.

That smile meant 'whatever you are doing at that moment had better cease.' My mother never abused us but she believed in running a house with what she called 'understanding.' We had to understand, although each one of my mother's children had a voice, there was a time to speak and a time to listen. We knew that she determined both of them.

With that said, my mother was a kind and very giving woman. But when we got out of line, she handled her business like she lived: hard and strong. We learned early on that there were repercussions for any of our actions. I was not yet eight years old, but I knew Mama was there to remind me to remain on the right side of the road. When it was too late for peace to be restored, the fake smile would disappear from Mama's face and all hell would break lose. She ran a stern house with love as its foundation.

We lived in an old colonial style home that had been in our family for generations. There were eight bedrooms; three upstairs and three downstairs, and two in the basement along with a half-bath. We had a formal living room and dining room as well and one of the largest kitchens I'd ever seen. We had one of the nicest yards on the block. Mama made sure of that. All of the houses on our street were kept up, but the same could not be said about the surrounding neighborhood.

Just a mile or two down the road, another way of life was in existence. By day the streets were filled with trash and human clutter. Both men and women refused to work whether they were qualified or otherwise. On any given day you could see more than two dozen crackheads out on the streets, scheming their next plan to feed their high.

On the southeast side of town, the place to be was Murphy's Park on the corner of Montgomery and Alexander, catty-corner from Nelly's Liquor Store. There was always the hottest dice game in town, a great dominoes game, and a street hooker. An old man named Benny sold hot links and barbecue sandwiches all day long. He attempted to oversee the madness that occurred in the middle of Murphy's Park.

Two blocks over was a well-known drug strip called Bernardo Lane. You could buy an ounce of crack cocaine, weed laced with PCP, uppers and downers, some rubies and some reds, or just about anything else to keep your addiction fed. There were your self-acclaimed pimps and your wanna be hustlers, your two-time losers and your first-time buyers.

The elderly had grown too afraid to come out of their houses and children could no longer play in their front yards. I was five years old when I saw my first shooting. Before my sixth birthday I saw my first murder. After seeing a man being shot down in cold blood, I wanted to run home as fast as I possibly could. But I was with a friend of mine named Melvin. He never seemed to care one way or the other about what he saw.

Someone attempted to hold back the wife of the dead man. She was fighting with all of her might to get free just to touch him one last time. A little boy was with her. He stood there frozen, seemingly unaware of the magnitude of what had just happened. He couldn't have been any older than me.

As they began to cover his father's face he had no expression on his own. He was motionless as he watched the men pick his father's body up and carry it away. He never moved. He never reached for comfort. He never cried one tear for the man who had been placed in his life to protect him.

I was hurting for him, but Melvin never seemed to lose his composure. His face was relaxed and unshaken by all of the madness. The screaming of those who had panicked around us did not move him. I was afraid and I wasn't afraid to say it. My knees were knocking like two rocks and my heart was pounding like a drum. I finally turned to run home.

Melvin said, "Nic, where are you going? Wait! Let's see them drive off. Where are you going, man? Look at all that blood. Isn't this crazy? It's like watching TV!"

A few years later I overheard my mother talking to an old friend of hers on the phone. I could tell the conversation was about my father. Standing outside her bedroom door was wrong, but I needed to know more. Every time someone talked about Malik I was intrigued. I had been taught not to interrupt grown-ups unless it was an emergency, and I had heard enough over the last fifteen or so minutes for this to be one. Mama was responding to her friend's story about someone who had seen Malik over on Third and McCarty about two years ago. That would have been about the time I heard his name in the store. Before I knew it, I pushed opened the door to my mother's bedroom.

"Mama, I thought you told me my father died when you were carrying me. Did you lie to me? Mama, you told me that it was wrong to lie."

She looked up at me with surprise and began to shake her head from side to side. I closed the door and headed towards my room.

I could hear her shouting out to me, "Nicoli! Nicoli, come back here!"

I was too hurt to stop. I could hear her footsteps as I ran to get to my bedroom. As soon as I was inside with the door locked she began to beat on the door as hard as she could.

"Baby, open up the door and let Mama talk to you," she pleaded.

I reluctantly opened the door for her. My chin was against my chest and I began to cry like I had never cried before.

"Nicoli, how long have you been listening to me talk on the phone?" She had shame written all over her face.

I ran across the room and dove onto my bed. I clutched my pillow with both hands and buried my head in it as deeply as I possibly could. Through tears of deception, I could feel my mother's hands begin to stroke the back of my neck. After a few moments I could feel our souls begin to caress each other's sorrows. The consoling of our hearts soon dried up the tears.

"Nicoli," she said. "Please don't be mad at me. I never wanted you to find out this way."

To my knowledge my mother had never lied to me before and I had always respected her for being painfully honest. The truths she spoke at times were hard to deal with.

"Son," she said pulling me close, "he never returned any of my calls. What was I supposed to do? What was I supposed to tell you?"

"The truth, Mama. Just the truth, like you've always done in the past. You should have told me the truth."

She still wasn't ready to deal with it, I could tell. I felt she was hurting twice as much as I was. I never asked her where Malik was, because something told me she didn't know.

When I first discovered that my father wasn't actually dead, an angry spirit began to fill the void that my father had left in my life. I was pushed into the world with my mother's love, but forced to live in it with so little hope. Since that day of discovery I was forever running from the streams that flowed to the waters of iniquity.

Malik must have felt that he lacked the basic human instinct required to be a parent. He kept his feet on the road of immaturity and not only walked away from his adult responsibilities, but he walked away from me. From birth, he allowed me to become a common statistic with less than a fifty-fifty chance of success.

I wonder what kind of man walks away from something as precious as a newborn child. What level of denial must one reach to successfully reject a part of himself? How can he still be able to maintain the mental aptitude necessary to live after committing such terrible degree of treason?

As children, we are not without thoughts, though many times we have problems articulating our truths. Many children learn to smile on the outside to mask the dull pain that comes from the unknown. We ask our parents to pay close attention to things that go unsaid. There are many lessons that can be learned in silence, for it has been written that still waters run deep.

A child who has always had a father could never understand what I was feeling. He has never known the hollowness of a fatherless soul. He may have experienced some form of family division, but not the total separation nor lack of inspiration that eats away at a fatherless child. If he has heard the rough sound of his father's voice or smelled the scent of his working clothes, he could never understand me.

I wasn't a disrespectful kid, but I had my moments and rebelled for the attention. I was jealous of any child who had a father in his home. I wasn't shy or ashamed to let the world know.

When my mother took me to the barbershop I would see other kids there with their dads. I would be overcome with sadness at that simple sight. My mother knew early on that I battled with what I now call 'fatherless-depression.'

My sisters all had the same father who died fighting cancer. My father lived for himself and he must have never seen anything worth dying for. I didn't know what to think knowing he was alive. Until now I had been dealing with a whole different set of circumstances and in a matter of seconds, after learning the truth, I was forced to deal with a brand new reality. My heart was pounding endlessly from opening a wound, which might never heal.

Who was I? Why was I forced to live in a world without being able to hear my father's voice? Why couldn't my father have been a hero? Why did he have to do those things equating to zero? I was angry with cowardly men who spoke so strong, yet walked so weak.

I made a vow to myself the day I found out Malik was still alive; I would never cause a woman to hurt like my mother had. Images of my father had become tainted and the happy descriptions that had once run through my soul were forever altered.

My emotions turned evasive and blocked the windows of my soul. I could only see out now. From then on any man who claimed to be a man would have to show me the physical credentials necessary to buy a moment of my time. From then on, I felt unworthy of love, especially the love that comes from a father. For the most part I was surrounded by love of my 'Four Queens,' but I hated living in this world without the love of my father. I stopped blaming my mother for my father's nonexistence though. I learned then that no one could be made to love.

As the years passed I could appreciate my sisters' qualities better, even though I was walking my own path. At age twenty-four, Taylor didn't look a day over eighteen. She's a very pretty lady and one day she's gonna make someone real happy. She has long, gorgeous hair, which she keeps tied up in a ponytail. She is about five-feet seven and has a body that is banging. That simply means that she could be a model in Penthouse, but because of her integrity, she prefers to be a teacher in the schoolhouse. She teaches at a high school on the other side of town. She has an outgoing personality and has always had a great head on her shoulders. She was never the kind of young lady who would fall for all the tricks that the niggas played in the streets. I grew to love her truthfulness and I knew that she would always give me the best advice possible.

That year Lauren was twenty-three. She is about five-eight and all ass. She has a wonderful smile and its radiance makes up for her small chest. She wears her hair short and neat and gets it cut once a week like clockwork. She's the most outgoing of us all being a people person who loves to converse with anyone who will listen. She is a paralegal and dates nothing but 'suits.' Her guys wear nothing but suits, period. She told me she couldn't have any less, and she'd never relinquish that requirement. She loved her 'suits' and as long as they made her happy, I was happy.

Rae was twenty-one, and still the quiet one of the bunch. She is a little slow because of complications at birth, my mother said. She looks normal, but her reactions aren't always on point. She never really had much to say, and we all protected her the best we could. Men would try to take advantage of her innocence and were often attempting to lure her into their cars.

She isn't the brightest young lady in the world but she wasn't no fool. She is just as fine as Taylor and Lauren. We just worried that her mind never caught up with her body. She is easy to approach, but harder to leave; yet her spirit is so warm.

Rae has always been there for me. She speaks so slowly and we learned we better not be in a hurry or have anywhere to go when we set down with her. She needed time to complete her sentences. All I knew was when the world insisted I make an appointment to speak my mind, Rae was taking walk-ins. I would often lay my head across her lap as she stroked my brow and listened to the things I had to say. She was and is my emotional sounding board. She is my brace when the world makes me weak. She is my confidante when I am lonely. If you didn't know her you would think she was sad. But Rae ain't sad. She just reserves her smiles. She keeps them stored for those moments when the ones she loves have somehow run out of them.

Another significant crossroads was impossible for me to ignore. Breaking through my struggles gave me the incentive to reach for more in life. I reopened the wounds that otherwise would have festered, and my 'Four Queens' helped me break away.

I was walking down the dark plague-ridden streets of madness. I released my moral stronghold when I learned the truth about my father. At that point in time I released my link in the family chain.

One day I woke up with my pants sagging and my character dragging. I lost the swagger of emotional stability that my mother had granted me since I was able to walk. I had lost respect for myself and it was getting harder to respect others. I needed to be in the company of fools in order to hide my true emotions.

I learned early in life that 'niggas' were different from Black people. I learned that Black people will do all it takes to make it, but niggas will do all they can to take it. A Black man will work and support his Black family and honor his Black queen. A nigga will disrespect his whole family along with its premise. He will keep his sorry ass home and ask his queen to support him and his children.

What did I do? I became a nigga. Hell, it was the easier of the two roads and I wasn't trying to work for nobody.

Allow me to introduce my niggas to you. My main nigga is Chuck. He weighs in at around two hundred pounds, which is a lot to support with a five-nine frame. The young ladies call him Big Chocolate, but Chuck is a matador of a nigga, and when it comes to bravery, hearts don't get no bigger. He's great with the ladies, and hands down one of the most successful back-beaters under the age of twenty-one. Chuck is good with his hands and is slowly becoming legendary on the block.

Stick, he's my up-the-street nigga. His name says it like it is. He is about six-four and his head never quite caught up with the rest of his body. He is so skinny that his belt almost wraps twice around his waist. I saw Stick hide behind a telephone pole once. Stick is a light-skinned nigga with absolutely no class. He was abandoned by his parents at four months old, and has been through just about every foster care system in the Northern Valley. He's not the brightest nigga in the world, but it ain't nothing at the age of twenty years old he ain't seen. I remember standing with Stick, when he was still called Marvin, the day we had just witnessed our first murder.

When it comes to keeping it real, Stick is the most real cat to ever put on a pair of shoes. He isn't afraid to tell you that he wasn't built for love. He is quick to remind anyone that will listen that he'd appreciate it if we didn't bring anyone that we truly loved around him.

If someone asks him why he says, "If she gives it to me, I'm gonna take it. So be real with yourself, nigga, and keep ya bitch away from me before I do her and start spending ya money." He'd laugh at himself even though the shit wasn't funny.

He'd say, "I ain't never gonna be loyal, because no matter what I say to my johnson, it rises at the first sight of freshness, and freshness ain't got no name." Despite these warnings, if I'm going anywhere I've got to take that nigga with me.

Do-Me, who is nearly twenty, is quite short for his age. He is different all the way around. Do-Me has a whole bunch of ain't gots. Do-Me ain't got no car. He ain't got no manners, and he ain't got no features to really speak on. Do-Me was the last to get everything. He is funny looking at best, but somehow he stays geared up and gets his hair cut every Friday. His hair, his walk, even the way he talks is delayed. He always sounds like he has a frog in his throat. Do-Me is a shit-talker and has mad rapping skills. He had a great smile, but he messed up and got some bad gold. Now the nigga ain't got no teeth.

I wasn't about to blame my current condition on becoming a nigga. But something prompted my mentality to change.

My Uncle Leon used to say, "Nicoli, come on let's be real. Just how many real niggas do you know who around the house listening to jazz music? He'd ask pointedly, "You don't believe that Rap music promotes violence and anger? Okay then, do me a favor. The very next time you're setting down watching Rap videos, just turn down the music and study the faces. Then tell me what message they're sending out."

Even though the majority of the lyrics were negative, I wasn't about to admit that it had any effect on my judgment. I felt that nothing could alter my understanding nor penetrate my rationality. I thought I was too damn strong and too damn right to become influenced by the lyrics. Almost every song I heard was suggesting that I remain angry, and I should have known the songs wanted me to conjure up internal anger that would provoke an even worse system. But I remained diligent in my listening.

My mother used to tell me, "Son, don't let that music change you, and don't let the ways of this world rearrange you."

I had listened to my queens all my life, but now none of their words could hold a candle to the wisdom that my cronies were spitting out. It wasn't just the music; it was the whole way of life. I was smoking weed at the age of ten and selling crack at the age of twelve.

When everyone was asleep, I'd sneak out of my window and do my dirt all night long. I did some of my homework as soon as I got home from school and slept until it got dark. This went on for some time until my mother found out that I was ditching school at least a couple days a week.

One day, my niggas and I were hanging out in front of the corner store a few streets over from where I lived. We had our own way of making hash, a high grade of marijuana, which we were trying to sell. Out of nowhere, Five-O came down on us. There had to have been at least four cars full of them.

I could hear Do-Me saying, "Throw the shit in here, throw the shit in here," as he pointed to a nearby trashcan.

Being the youngest at seventeen I was given the weed and tried to throw it away. I got caught red-handed, but I really didn't care. I got points for taking one for the team and the stripes on my nigga jacket had just multiplied.

I knew that I was embarrassing my queens, who by that time seemed ready to cut their losses. I was being embraced by the street niggas by letting go of my family. I was learning to tune out the world.

No one in my family had ever done drugs but I was coming home higher than the Statute of Liberty. I was running with the kind of niggas who didn't believe in justice. My life as I knew it was gone and there were times when I even scared myself.

The niggas I hung out with were intimidators who terrorized the community just because. We were dangerous, not only to ourselves, but to society. We called ourselves G.A.B., for Guilty At Birth. We believed that no matter what we did, we were always gonna be guilty of something. So we came up with G.A.B. We were troublemakers by our own admission and we had no premonitions of living better lives. Since birth, trouble was all we knew, and now trouble was all we were.

One day we were all sitting around, just shooting the shit, smoking some bomb-ass weed that Do-Me had picked up early that morning. Something was strange about that high and I didn't ask for a second take. But Chuck, Stick and Do-Me kept on smoking until they started tripping out.

"What is this shit we smoking on Do-Me?" asked Chuck.

"Man, this is the Chronic," he informed us.

"Nigga, I been smoking Chronic for ten years and I ain't never felt like this," said Stick.

It wasn't three minutes later when a man came riding down the street. Do-Me said, "Damn look at that pencil riding that bicycle." The weed had them hallucinating and I was laughing my ass off.

Chuck, who was always so damn cool, had lost his smoothness somewhere after his first hit. Rasheeda, the neighborhood ho who Chuck hated with a passion, was coming up the street towards us. Chuck shouted,

"Hey old fine bitch, what is yo name?"

Rasheeda knew that something was wrong with him because Chuck had never come at her that way.

"What are you suckers smoking?" she asked. "Whatever it is, ya'll don't ever need to smoke that shit again."

"Bitch, this shit is the Chronic, don't you know?" asked Stick.

She just kept on walking and shaking her head.

Stick was too afraid to move. He kept looking down at his legs claiming that one of them was gone. "One of my legs is gone, nigga can't you see?"

"No, old skinny ass nigga, you've got both of your legs. It's just that both of them are together and your ass is so damn skinny, they just look like one leg." We all laughed until we couldn't laugh anymore. Stick didn't think it was funny. He just kept on feeling for his other leg.

Two days later we found out that joint we had smoked was laced with PCP and it was supposed to be a practical joke played on Do-Me. We never again smoked anything that Do-Me had without being there with him when he purchased it. It was dreadful to think about some of the crazy shit we did. A lot of the things were so shallow and scandalous.

We imprisoned our minds by believing that we all were inferior. We were taught that we were worthless, not just by our families, but also by the things we saw on TV. We never doubted each other's abilities; we just never took the time to help nourish them.

We were all envious of someone, whether we wanted to believe it or not. Stick was betrayed by both of his parents and seemed to be envious of everyone with a family. Chuck was deceived by his mother, who chose to love everyone else but him, simply because he looked so much like his father. Do-Me was smarter than he appeared. He was a lot of lip-service, but he knew how to manipulate the system.

All of my friends laughed at me for revealing that I chose to remain celibate. I was always being chastised, and the gang would tease me about never doing it. I told them that I wanted to get myself together before I had sex and got someone pregnant. One day after I said that for about the hundredth time, Do-Me reached into his pocket and pulled out a package of rubbers.

"Nigga, have you ever heard of these?" he asked.

"Sure I have," I said and shuffled my feet. I had only touched a condom at school during sex education, but I couldn't tell my niggas that.

"Damn, Nic, don't ya ever get hard?" asked Stick.

"Hell yeah, nigga. What do you think, I'm human ain't I?"

"I don't know, my brother. All the humans I know your age are doing it, so to me something is wrong. What the hell are you waiting on, my brother?"

"I just don't want to bring a child into this world and not take care of it, like my father did me."

"I heard that, my brother," said Stick.

"You do what you gotta do, and I do what I gotta do, and I'm gon get me some. And if you knew what I did about these bitches, you'd get you some and call it a day on that old moralistic bullshit you're screaming," said Chuck.

I never took anything that they said personally, but it was starting to get to me. I knew I wasn't gonna kick nobody's ass or anything like that. That is not as long as Chuck was running the show. This was their way of humbling me and getting me ready for the evil tasks that still lie ahead.

One night while cruising around, smoking and listening to some one of Chuck's partners had made, we noticed our rival's cars parked in front of a local hamburger joint on the corner of Fifth and Mercer. Stick saw them first.

"No. Them niggas ain't hanging out over here! We don told them to keep their asses out of our neighborhood. Chuck, pull this damn car over and let me have a word with these selective-memory-having suckers."

That was the first night of real trouble for me. I had always heard about real violence but this was about to be some major shit jumping off. When we first pulled up to 'Tasty Burger,' my heart was racing a mile a minute and my hands were sweating like I had the flu. Once again I was too damn afraid to admit that I was afraid. I loved these niggas too much to punk-out on them.

We parked across the street behind a dumpster and got out of the car. Chuck and Stick were veterans at this shit and Do-Me just didn't care. They had guns hidden underneath a fake tire inside the trunk. As they got them out, I was pulling myself together for the madness that was about to take place.

Stick looked at me and said, "Little nigga, you ready for some real shit?"

I nodded my head as he placed a nine-millimeter in my hand.

"Brace yourself and watch your ass. If you get scared, stand behind me and you'll be fine. 'Cause you see, they can't kill me cause I'm already dead."

Chuck looked over at me and said, "I told you that his ass was crazy, didn't I?"

Do-Me was puffing on a joint, which was hanging on the end of his big lips. He held a gun in each hand. "Shit, let's do these sons-of-bitches," he said.

Chuck was still as cool. "Niggas let's do this shit right or die wrong," he cautioned.

I really didn't know what that meant but it seemed to fire everybody up, so much so that, hell, I even started yelling. One of the rival members came out by himself, walking with a broad who used to do Chuck a while back. By the way Chuck acted, he hadn't really gotten over her.

"No. Tell me that nigga ain't trying to come over here," he said. "Stay right here niggas, and watch my back."

We watched as they walked around towards the girl's car. She sat in the driver's seat and reached over to let him in. Just as they started talking, Chuck opened the passenger door and pulled the nigga out of the car. The girl started screaming and Chuck said, "Bitch take your trifling ass home before I shoot you."

Chuck pulled that nigga back across the street at gunpoint and placed him against the car.

"I thought I told you to never bring your ass back over on this side of the tracks," he snarled.

"You did nigga, but I go wherever the hell I wanna go."

Chuck knocked out five of his teeth with the butt of his gun.

"Damn, nigga," said Stick. "I wish that nigga was my bitch right about now, 'cause I bet from this point on, he's gonna be able to suck a mean dick."

I had never been so close to anger, nor had I ever been able to smell it in the air; not like I could at that very moment. How could they be laughing while this man's teeth were rolling around on the ground? It wasn't two minutes later that four or five of his boys came out looking for him. Chuck and Do-Me had him in our car with his hands tied behind his back. There was an old washrag stuffed into his mouth.

He tried to get their attention so Stick opened up the left side passenger door and knocked him out. Do-Me walked over to them and said their partner went with some girl. He left word that he would get back with them later. They believed Stick and before too long got into their cars and pulled off.

Our plan was to follow them and leave our own message. At least that is what Chuck and Stick said, but I really didn't know what they meant. While we were following them, the dude came to. Still bleeding from the mouth and now from his left ear, he just sat there looking helpless, staring off into space. My guess is he was just hoping to stay alive.

When we made a left turn the dude's head would touch Do-Me's shoulder and Do-Me would say, "Get ya big ass head off my shoulder." He pushed him back up into a straight position.

How did Do-Me think that he was supposed to keep his head straight without his hands free to balance himself?

"What are we going to do with this nigga?" asked Stick.

"Well, we're going to blind this nigga so that he won't ever be able to identify us," Chuck said.

I thought that they were playing, but Stick thought that it was the most ingenious solution he had ever heard.

He said, "Damn dog, that's some Mafia shit there. I've always wanted to be hard-core like one of them Mafia dudes. Let me cut the nigga's eyes out, that's my kinda shit."

A few minutes later, Chuck made a left turn. Do-Me had just taken a hit off his joint and when the dude's head hit his shoulder again, it made him drop his joint in his lap. Before anyone knew it, Do-Me shot the sorry nigga in the head.

"Nigga, what the fuck is wrong with your ass?" asked Chuck.

They were obviously disappointed that Do-Me had just killed a man in their presence, but all Chuck said was, "Fool, now I've got to get my car detailed again. I just got it washed last week."

Stick turned around and looked at Do-Me. "Damn, Do-Me! That was crazy. But I guess if you gon do some crazy shit, that's the top of the line."

There I was, sitting in the car with three fools who apparently had lost their minds and were now trying to make me lose mine. Chuck turned into an alley and pulled the dead dude out of the car and onto the ground. He turned the music up loud and began to move his head up and down, back and forth, acting as if nothing had happened.

Stick reached over and turned down the music. "Damn, ain't ya'll hungry?" he asked.

Do-Me said, "Hell yeah, I thought you niggas were on a diet or something." I had just witnessed a murder and there they were talking about food.

We went back over to our side of town. Not once did anyone say a word about the man Do-Me had killed just twenty minutes ago. When we stopped, Stick collected all the guns and placed them back into the secret place. I was feeling like a bitch inside, but I couldn't break down. I couldn't show that I was against what had happened that night.

I finally graduated two months later from high school and to this day, I don't know how I did it. Towards the end of my senior year I was hardly ever there. But I knew that finishing school would make my queens happy.

On graduation night, I remember looking over at my family wondering where my niggas were. I knew they wouldn't be sitting next to my queens, but I wanted them there to support me.

After the ceremony, my mother walked over and hugged me. She whispered into my ear, "Son, I am very proud of you. Now it's time for you to become proud of yourself. I love you with all my heart and soul, Nicoli. But you won't make it another year living this way."

We went to a nearby restaurant to celebrate. It was just the 'Four Queens' and me. I knew the day would come when they would all have something to say about the way that I had been living. This was the day, and for the moment I respected them enough to listen. Taylor led off with tears in her eyes.

"Nic, I don't know what you're searching for out there in those streets, but if it's love, it's right here. Why are you so afraid of us Nic?"

"Why do you think that I'm afraid of something?"

"Why? Because for whatever reason you won't face anything. Nic, you're gonna die in those streets if you don't learn that there's something worth living for inside of you."

Lauren took it from there. "Nic, you've just received one of the last free things this world has to offer."

"And what is that?"

"A free education," Lauren replied simply.

"So is life gonna give me something else for free?"

"Our love, you fool! The love from your 'Four Queens' has always been free."

I turned to look at my youngest sister, Rae, as tears were running down her face.

"Why are you crying, Rae?" I asked.

I will never forget the way she responded. She took her right hand and pointed towards the tears. She said, "These are just a few of the tears I've shed for you, my brother. I miss talking to you about your troubles. I've heard you tell people over the years that I was slow. I know that you thought you were saying it low enough so I wouldn't hear you, but I heard you Nic. Let me just say this, I might not be very quick to speak, but one thing is for sure I'm not slow. When you used to leave the house before me and leave the iron on, who do you think cut it off? If you wondered how you finished school when you were barely there, I had done your homework and slipped it back into your book bag. Nic, I love you so much, but you're too slow to see that! The reason you don't see more tears is because my soul is tired of worrying about yours."

By that time all of my queens were crying and I stood corrected. We joined hands as Taylor led us in a prayer before we ate our dinner. After we ate I thanked them all for their support and told them all that I loved them. I said that I would try to do better.

The way Rae spoke moved me. It was like she had the key to my heart and had opened it up and filled it with promise. Rae never said another word to me that night but after dinner she came over to hug me. She touched my face with her left hand, pausing for only a second. Then she smiled as she walked away.

If they only knew all the things that I had done up to that point, they'd probably still be screaming at me. I'm sure they had heard things about me out there in the streets but none of them ever said anything to me about what I was doing. Lauren was right though, wasn't nothing free anymore.

Do-Me had just gotten himself locked up on some credit card charges. Apparently he had been taking them off department store counters and running them up to their limits. He was facing a lot of time and so was Stick, Chuck and me.

The girl at the burger joint had followed us to the other side of town that night and told the police that we had killed Jermil Lewis, a.k.a. Nasty. They called him that because of the nasty shit he kept stirring up. Chuck didn't know it, but we had all just played a role in murdering the father of that girl's baby.

Along the way we had become notorious for doing crazy shit. Two days after Do-Me shot Nasty in the head, we robbed a small convenient store about four miles away from where we lived. It was Stick's idea. He knew that before the murder I was fresh. They all figured that a 'clean man' would rat under pressure, if he were ever to be interrogated. Robbing that store was supposed to discourage me from doing so.

We were all getting high before the robbery, but not like we did when Do-Me was with us. He always kept the joint longer than anyone else, so this time it seemed like there was more to go around. We were taking fifths of Hennessey to the head as we pulled into the parking lot.

When we first walked into the store my legs were shaking like leaves on a tree. I was reaching for my composure, but it seemed to be too damn far away to touch. Chuck went to the back of the store to see if the store clerk was alone. I was supposed to wait for him to give me a signal that the coast was clear.

I was standing near the chips when I got the sign from Chuck. I pulled down the rack when Chuck nodded his head. The clerk came from behind the counter and when he bent over to pick up the chips I busted him over the back of his head with the butt of a gun. It was the same gun that Do-Me had used in the murder and now my prints were all over it. The man laid there unconscious while Stick ran behind the counter and opened the cash register. I just stood there hoping he wasn't dead, while at the same time wishing that I was.

Chuck ran towards the front of the store and looked outside. He started screaming, "Come on! Let's get the hell out of here! The police are coming!"

Something was seriously wrong with Stick. Knowing the police were coming, he still ran and grabbed two half racks of beers. He finally ran out of the store shooting at what appeared to be a hidden camera. There were sirens all around us and we had just enough time to get out of the store and turn the corner before they arrived.

When we first got back into the car Chuck was going off on Stick's ass saying, "You crazy nigga, what are you trying to do, get us caught?"

We had a place to go cool down and chill out. A place back off in the cut where no one in the neighborhood knew us. One of Chuck's broads, Pam, stayed there. She had a sister who lived with her and had always told Chuck that she liked me. Stick and Chuck told me to stay there with Pam and her sister. At first I felt uncomfortable, but when I saw Tamara I felt they had made the right decision leaving me there. There was every indication my days of celibacy were over.

"We're going to J.W.'s house to get rid of the guns. That nigga takes care of hot items like these," Stick announced.

When they left I went into the bathroom. When I came out I saw one of the bangingest broads ever. She was about five-six and built like a goddess. She had on a pair of jeans that must have taken her hours to put on. Her hair was cut short into one of those neat styles that drives niggas crazy. If she were an ice-cream cone, I would say that she had been dipped twice into beauty and once into grace. I stood there at a loss for words. I had never seen such splendor.

"So, we finally meet," she said with a smile.

I didn't know how to respond, so I just smiled back.

"Well, aren't you gonna say anything to my little sister?" asked Pam.

"I was just thinking about how much you two look alike." They both just stared at me. "Well, is that a bad thing or what?"

Pam continued with introductions. "This is my sister, Tamara, and Tamara, this is Nicoli."

"I've seen you many times, but I never had the pleasure of meeting you," I said.

Tamara responded, "Shit, the pleasure is all mine. Would you like something to drink, Nicoli?"

I almost lost the strength in both of my knees when she turned around and walked into the kitchen. She had everything, and I mean everything.

Tamara came back wearing a great big smile on her face and carrying my drink in her hand. "I didn't know how much ice you took, so I hope it's okay," she said as she offered me my drink.

She didn't know that by that time she could have given me a Big Gulp straw and lead me to her bathroom. I would have been fine just drinking her bath water with or without ice.

Tamara attempted to take full advantage of the time we had alone.

"Why do you seem so nervous?" she asked. "My sister is in the other room and she's cool. Loosen up. Come over here and have a seat next to me. It's getting a little cold and I need you to keep me warm."

I was starting to feel things I never felt before in my life. I knew that it wouldn't be long before we would get caught and I didn't want to go to prison a virgin. I began taking my drinks to my head and said, "Would you like to smoke a joint?"

"Shit, I thought you'd never ask."

"Didn't they tell you? I'll do anything with you. I've liked you for quite some time, but you always seemed to be looking the other way when my sister and I came by to see Chuck."

After a couple more drinks, she took me by the hand and led me into her bedroom. She stopped just before we got there and asked, "Are you sure you want me?" She rubbed her hands across my chest and kissed me.

I knew that Chuck and Stick had told her I'd never had sex before, but that really didn't bother me. Tamara was so fine. Hell, first time, last time, I wanted them all to be with her.

She instructed, "Sit down and listen to the music for a while. I'll be right back."

I wasn't going anywhere! I didn't care if the house was to catch on fire. A few minutes later Tamara walked back through the door wearing a see-through gown.

"I couldn't find my panties, I hope you don't mind."

I just sat there trying to cover up my sudden stiffness, which was growing harder by the second.

"No. Hell no, I don't mind. Damn girl, you're fine."

She walked over slowly and reached for my hand. I gave her my left hand, which she placed on her breast. The moment was drawing near and I felt that it was only fair that she knew.

"Tamara, I have never..."

She placed her hand over my mouth preventing me from delivering my confession.

She whispered, "I know. Don't worry, I won't hurt you. Take off your clothes and let me see you, pretty boy. I love opening new gifts, don't you?"

When she unzipped my pants she exclaimed, "Damn Nic, is all of this ya own? You might be starting late but believe me when I say this, if all of this is you, you're way ahead of the game."

She removed the rest of my clothes and pushed against my chest. I reached back to catch myself as I fell on the bed. She straddled me and the things she did with her tongue mesmerized me. As she continued to move down my body towards her destination, she said, "Brace yourself. Feel free to let go at anytime. There's no time limit on pleasure, Nicoli."

When she placed my head inside her mouth, her magical tongue began to rotate. It seemed that I had lived for eighteen long years in a world that felt like hell on earth, but for that brief moment I was in heaven. My niggas were always telling me that having your dick sucked was a beautiful thang. I couldn't wait to slap the shit out of someone for not making me do this shit sooner.

Tamara asked in a sexy voice, "Nic, do you like the way I do this?"

I thought the arch in my back along with my toes curling up would have already answered that question but all I could say was, "No, don't stop!"

"Well, how's your first piece?" She wanted more information.

If I could have said anything I would have already said it. I just concentrated on things that would keep me from nutting; like the times when I got in trouble for stealing an old lady's purse over at the mall, or about all those times I got arrested for petty crimes as a kid. My recollection of those things had gotten me past the ten-minute mark but penetration was distorting my memory. She knew that I was about to come and she had the nerve to speed up her movements. I was feeling helpless, like a little nigga strapped in a stroller being pulled by a runaway locomotive.

My eyes were blinking on their own, and my hands were full of ass.

"Nic, tell me when you get ready to nutt."

I thought this was crazy. "Righttttt Nnoowwww!" I hollered.

"Tell me how it feels," she purred.

While reaching for what little composure I had left inside of me I breathed, "Emp-ty."

I had nothing to compare to my first time experience, but something told me that mine had to have been one of the best. After we were through, Tamara wanted me to hold her. She pressed her big butt up against me and was reached back for my hand. I had never caressed anyone before, but after what she had just done for me, I was willing to try.

"There, now doesn't this feel good?" she murmured.

I thought 'of course,' but if she didn't move her ass out of the way I was gonna start poking at it in a few more minutes.

It wasn't thirty minutes later when we heard a loud knock on the bedroom door.

"Who is it?" asked Tamara.

"It's me," Pam said. "Come here for a second."

Tamara got up and told me she would be right back. Pam told her that Chuck had called and said that we were all over the news. They had put an APB out on us and were running the story on every local station in town. Tamara came back and sat on the edge of the bed. She told me what was going on.

"Nic," she said, "holding up that store was wrong. Your face is all over the news. What are you gonna do?"

"What options do I have? I've just got to lay low until Chuck and Stick come to get me."

Pam ran back into the room and said, "They got him! They've caught Big Chocolate!"

I jumped out of the bed butt naked and reached for my clothes. Pam was still in the room and said, "Damn, Tamara," as if she was cold and I was a pot of hot coffee. "You might wanna harbor that nigga for awhile. Ain't no sense in having all that locked up."

She turned to me and said, "Damn, Nic. You mean to tell me that you is just getting around to using that thang?"

"Pam, leave him alone. He's got a lot on his mind."

"Yeah, and about thirty or forty minutes ago, you had a lot of his mind in you."

When Pam closed the door, Tamara tried to calm me down.

"Now you have to have a plan, Nic. You have to turn yourself in. They've got you on camera Pam says, and it doesn't look good. If they have to find you, you won't get a deal. They'll put ya ass underneath the jailhouse."

She was right. I was tired of running and it was time for me to pay for all the dirt I had done.

"Damn, can I use your phone, Tamara?"

"Sure, it's over there on the side of the bed."

"Where? I didn't hear it when Chuck called."

"Oh, I turn it off when I don't want to be bothered."

"That's something to remember."

I called my mother who had been worrying about me for hours. I knew that my queens had seen me on the news and I planned to call them too.

"Nic, where are you son?" Mama asked. "Everyone's over here and we are all going through it. You've got to turn yourself in at once. The police have been looking for you boys everywhere. I saw you on the news, son, hitting that man over the head. What has gotten into you boy? You weren't raised like that!" She sounded frantic.

"I know, Mama. I just fucked my life up, that's all."

It sounded like she dropped the phone out of frustration, or she just couldn't stand to hear my voice anymore. Lauren got on the phone next and let me have it. "Nicoli, Nicoli, didn't I tell you that wasn't nothing else gonna be free?"

"Yes, you did Lauren, but I didn't listen."

My queens had been losing me since I was ten, and now they felt they had finally lost me for good. I gathered myself for what I deserved. Rae had to say her peace.

"Nicoli, why did you turn your back on our love? Where are your nigga friends now that you need them the most? I've been waiting to talk to you again every since graduation. Now it seems like you'll never truly be able to graduate from the school that matters the most," she said.

"Well, what school is that, Rae?"

"The school of life, my brother. You're getting ready to do some hard time. Maybe by the time you get home, you will have slowed down enough to spend some quality time with your slow sister. Turn yourself in and pay the price. Maybe one day your heart and soul might be as one. I love you Nicoli. Good-bye."

Tamara saw that the phone conversation was getting to me. While I was talking she got up and fixed me another drink.

"Here Boo, drink this and get that shit off your mind. Roll with it."

She leaned over and kissed my forehead and then walked her fine self over to the other side of the room and accidentally dropped something.

Hell, I knew that it was just a matter of time before I was in prison, so I did like Tamara suggested and started to roll with it. I took the drink and started thinking about what Tamara and I had already done. When she turned around, it must have looked like there was a tent set up in the middle of the bed.

She turned around and saw what was happening. "Now Nic, did you reach over on the side of my bed to get my bat, or what?"

"Hey, just put your head underneath the covers for a minute. I've got something for you to stare at," I told her. She turned off the lights and we had sex all through the night.

When the sun began to touch the window I got up to look outside. There was a strange car parked across the street. I had run out of time. I could smell a pig from two miles away and the scent of pork was more evident now than ever.

Tamara was still asleep. I didn't want my troubles to awaken her, so I put on my clothes as silently as possible. I walked over and kissed her forehead and made sure that she was completely covered.

At the front door I said a short prayer. *"Father, protect me from the danger ahead and forgive me for all the harm I have caused."*

I opened the door, walked through, and closed it slowly behind me. I knew I was being watched and that I needed to surrender, not only to the police, but also to God. I took a couple of steps out into the streets and laid my face down on the cold pavement. Less than twenty seconds later I heard boots pounding towards my body.

"Police! Police! Keep your head down and spread your legs!"

Even though I was already down in the street, there were those who felt compelled to kick me and beat away at my already surrendered body. I later found out that they had spotted Pam's car, Chuck's getaway vehicle, by helicopter. They traced the registration and located me here at Pam's.

After placing me in handcuffs they pulled me up from the street. One of the cops walked over and hit me in the back of my head with his gun.

"Now you little thug, how does it feel to be hit in the back of the fucking head?"

While riding to the station, I was asked what seemed like a million questions. I refused to answer anything until I saw a lawyer. I knew I was facing twenty years in the penitentiary for armed robbery. I stayed locked up for eight months before going to court and it only took them eight days to find me guilty. I was to be sentenced within a month and I will never forget that day.

The jailor allowed me to peek through the glass in the door while the courtroom was being filled. I could see my queens coming in through the double doors at the front of the courtroom. It was evident mother had grown weak over the past several months. I could feel her tears dripping into my soul as she cried openly. With Taylor and Lauren by her side she had come to hear how many years her baby was going to receive. I was guilty of the crime in question but nothing had prepared me for what was to come.

When everyone was seated, I was led into the courtroom. When the judge came in my heart stopped beating for a moment. For the rest of the proceedings I felt myself gasping for air.

"Mr. Walker, will you please stand?" commanded the judge. "You have been found guilty of armed robbery. Do you have anything to say before I hand down your sentence before this court?"

It was quiet enough to hear a church mouse walking on cotton.

I knew that I was sorry for my crimes I had committed and said, "Yes Sir, I do. First of all, I would like to apologize to our victim, Mr. Moritz, for my violent behavior on the night in question. I know that my actions were wrong and that a debt has to be paid. All of this madness started the day that I found out my own father was still alive. I hated every man I could and started hating myself as well. When you send me to prison, you will only be closing the door to my cell, because several years ago, I imprisoned myself with the premise of anger.

"My queens never stopped loving me. It was I who rejected their love and reached out to caress anger. It was I who allowed this nigga spirit to come in and molest my soul. My queens had always taught me to be a stand-up guy. So today I stand before you, with the spirit of atonement reeking through my pores." I took a deep breath to hold back my tears. "Judge, I have one more thing to add. May I?"

The judge looked over at the prosecution's table and when they gave their okay he looked back over at me and said, "One more thing and be brief, Mr. Walker."

"I hope the years that I spend in prison will help you, Mr. Mortiz, in your healing process. Please do not think of all young Black men as you think of me, for even as I speak, somewhere in America, a young Black man is reaching for a higher level. I wish to not only tell you that I'm sorry, but I wish to also tell my Black community that

I'm sorry for the way I represented them. Thank you for letting me speak, Judge."

I stood there as the bailiff handed the judge an envelope. When he opened it he said, "Well I am disappointed that you chose to remain silent throughout this trial. Deep down you seem to have the potential of being a very nice person. But it was your aggravated actions that have brought us all here today. This is a part of the process that pains me to no end, but it is one that has to take place. A wrong has occurred and the only thing to do is try and right it. Mr. Walker, this court is sentencing you to not less than five years in the state penitentiary and your time there will not exceed eighteen years."

When the sentence was read, I could sense my mother reaching for me. She cried out openly, "No, nooooo! That's my baby! Please don't take h-h-himmm awayyy!"

I had shown very little emotion during the whole course of the trial, and I knew that if I turned to look at my queens, I wouldn't be able to keep my composure. Taylor and Lauren were there for my mother. Now I had to be there for myself. My tears held the only source of strength I had, so I never looked back as they shackled me and led me from the courtroom.

Chuck, Do-Me and Stick were all facing the three-strike mandatory prison sentence. They had all been out on parole with rap sheets a mile longer than most of the notoriously badass niggas we knew. Their murder trial came before the armed robbery trial, so they didn't have to deal with that case for a while yet. They were all found guilty. The girl at the burger joint testified she only saw three men in the car with Nasty and none of my niggas gave me up, thank God!

Chuck and Stick got twenty-five years for being accessories to murder. Do-Me was facing murder-one for being the actual shooter. It is a capital offense and punishable by the death.

About a week after my sentencing date I finally came to a place that I would come to know as my home. There had to have been twenty-five of us on the bus for crimes that ranged from stealing, to molesting children, to rape and murder. On the way there the bus was extremely quiet. It seemed like everyone was getting mentally ready to do his time. It was early in the morning when we arrived. The early summer sun appeared to be touching the trees on the southeast side of the penitentiary. There was barbed wire topped with razor wire as far as the eye could see.

We had all heard stories about prison life, but nothing we were ever told would be able to compare to being there. When the bus stopped we were all instructed to get off and form a single file line. There was a hardheaded nigga I came to know as Boosty, who was taking his time getting off the bus.

"Well, you see there's always gonna be a 'Tester,'" said the head jailer. "So this is how we greet them."

Everyone was standing outside in a single file line, as we were told, everyone but Boosty. The jailor motioned to another officer to release one of the dogs, a big German shepherd. They obviously thought it was an appropriate time to send us all a message.

The dog ran on the bus. Apparently he had been trained just for occasions like these. When Boosty saw the dog coming he ran towards the back of the bus, but the dog reached him in a split second and bit Boosty on the ass. Boosty screamed like the bitch he finally became as the dog pulled his ass off the bus.

I knew not to show any emotion, after all there were two more dogs with their eyes trained on us. When the dog stopped biting Boosty, he stood there with a look of embarrassment on his stupid face.

"Now that everyone's off the bus, let's go home girls," the jailer said.

We were led down a tunnel that had no doubt been designed to place fear inside our hearts. We walked for what seemed like miles through the corridors of listening to grown men making obscene gestures. The doors were colored coded to match different levels of crime. I could deal with the shouting, but the clanging of cell doors clanking one after another bothered me the most. The dreadful sound of doors opening and closing, and my not having a key to unlock them instantly began to eat away at me.

I was placed in a jail cell on the third floor of B-block with an old Gee who called himself Flesh-Wound. At first sight he appeared to be a madman who hadn't yet been diagnosed by a legal psychiatrist. I must admit that I was afraid to be locked up in a cell with him. He could see that I was green, so much so that if you planted me in the ground I would grow. I noticed a lot of books on his side of the cell.

I got up the nerve to ask, "Hey mister, how long have you been reading?"

He lifted his head from his book and said, "I've been reading something constructive since the day they locked me up."

I was sitting on the top bunk but before I knew it I jumped down to talk. "Old nigga, what's so constructive about reading?"

There was a moment of silence before he responded. "How long did they give you?"

"I got fifteen years, why?"

"Well, Youngster, make that the last time you ever use that word around me. If you ever fix your mouth to call me a nigga again, I will cut your tongue out and shove it so far up your ass it will be able to taste your intestines."

I gulped and knew that I was dealing with a whole new set of rules.

"Damn, I'm sorry, man, I didn't say that to piss you off."

"Do you know why there is so much fear inside your eyes at this very second?" I couldn't answer. "Well, I'll tell you why. For years you have been able to say things and haven't had to really deal with the consequences of your actions. Am I right?"

"Well, I guess so."

"Well, all of that is over. This is the real world. This world that you're getting ready to live in is a world with major repercussions for every move. Do you know what I'm saying to you, youngster? You have to learn the laws of the land or you will reap the negative consequences due a disobedient fool."

"Okay. Teach me the laws."

First he taught me to never mess with the 'Three-Gee's.' That meant don't mess with the Guards, don't Gamble, and don't fuck with the Gays. He taught me how to play card games with dominoes. There was a lot of prison terminology to soak up, so I turned myself into a human sponge.

"Youngster, you've got to listen to me well. I've been in this cell longer than you have been alive."

Flesh-Wound was about six-three and weighed over three hundred pounds. He ran his cellblock and almost everything else in the penitentiary. He spent countless hours with me teaching me how to fight. I learned that I should never do so without 'placing on my pistols.' That was almost like what boxers do to prepare their hands for a fight. I was never supposed to fight without wrapping up my hands. We needed to do this just in case some commotion jumped off. Something like some exchanging of blows. That way, when the guard asked to check our hands, they wouldn't be bleeding or be messed up. No fight evidence or after-effects.

The only way you could fight was to catch the square, which meant that you had to go out into the center of the cellblock and get down. You always had someone watching out for the man, so that the fight wouldn't bring any heat on our tank, our block. Every tank had a tank spokesman. Flesh-Wound was ours. He was the best at laying hands on people. He was a problem-solver. He would let you know who you could rob and who you couldn't.

Flesh-Wound lived good on the inside, better they say than anyone they'd ever seen do time. Wartime was the term used when it was time to hold court, and no one hit harder than Flesh. He once hit a brother so hard that two or three brothers who were watching him started crying for the man he hit. He hit with a crossover and damn near knocked the left side of his face off. For the most part he seemed a pleasant man, but when it was wartime, a group of armored cars couldn't stop him.

I once saw him take a man by his hair and write the word 'flesh' with his blood on the side of a wall. When he got through he walked back into our cell, took his pistols off, grabbed a book and started reading. All of that in a matter of two and a half minutes.

I saw a man get pushed off of the third floor once and nobody even blinked an eye. I've seen many brothers get shanked while incarcerated, and some of them were just left there to die. I lived on the third floor of hell and was taught how to exist while inside the fiery walls of endless animosity. I thanked Flesh daily for protecting my life. He didn't seem to like anyone else but me, and I never saw him talking to too many other people. One night he sat down and began to tell me why he was in prison.

"I know you've probably heard stories about why I'm here kid. Well straight out I killed a man once with my bare hands for disrespecting my space."

My heart was pounding. He looked over and caught me turning my back to the wall. I was trying to tuck the cover in all around me.

"Ain't no homosexual shit ever gon be allowed up in here, so don't you worry about that, Youngster."

Man did I feel relieved. I relaxed as he continued his story.

"Youngster, I was sentenced to ninety-nine years and a black day." I felt quizzical. "By the look on your face, I can tell you've never heard of such a thing. Well my guess is, after serving ninety-nine years I would have to then serve a black day, meaning an eclipse. They gave me that black day because they knew that most niggas ain't never seen an eclipse. I don't think that even if I were to live long enough to do the ninety-nine years I would ever see the black day. I don't watch TV nor do I read the newspapers, because both of them remind me that I'm not free.

"The anger that you smelled while on the outside will become intensified in here. What yo mama couldn't do in the first eighteen years of your life, this penitentiary will force you to do over night. Brace yourself and keep your eyes focused at all times. Sleep when you can, but never while you're standing in the midst of evil. What I will teach you is what I didn't learn myself. If I ever see that you no longer adhere to my wisdom, the sound of my voice will become mute to your ears."

Flesh-Wound was a poetic man who basically cared about my future. He knew deep down inside he would never be free as far as society was concerned, so he became free inside himself.

"Youngster, let me show you how to do some time."

We were walking in the yard one day and looking out amongst the trees. When Flesh-Wound said, "Youngster do you see those trees over yonder to your right?" I turned my head in that direction.

"Yes, Flesh-Wound, I see them. Why do you ask?"

"Now try to look at them without turning your head," he challenged.

"Shit, that's impossible."

"Yeah, I know. That's the way I do time. I'm always looking straight ahead. As long as I am focused, it's hard to get distracted. I've done twenty-some-odd years this way. Now you try it."

After hearing it put that way, I began to walk like the only man who dared to teach me anything worth knowing. I kept my mind on positive things, occupying it with what I had absorbed over the years from Flesh-Wound. I never let the evil that surrounded my soul interrupt my program again.

All through the nights I could hear inmates being raped, beat down and even stabbed. There were numerous suicide attempts, sometimes two or three a week. Flesh–Wound taught me how to turn down the volume of madness and how to be still while the rage of death was festering in the air. No one ever stepped to me wrong while I was in prison, because Flesh-Wound was the man. I guess that was God's way of looking out for me, since my queens were nowhere around.

I would get cards from them from time to time, but they were often too damn sad to read. They made sure that I had money on my books so that I could get the things I needed from the commissary. I had pictures of my queens taken on the night of my high school graduation.

I had been in prison almost four years before I knew it. I had disconnected myself from the free world as I knew it, in order to do the time that was still ahead of me. There were people who were in jail while in jail. They were doing their time when they caught another case. I've met brothers who came in doing three years and ended up serving a life sentence. There was no such thing as rehabilitating or reforming while being incarcerated.

I came up for parole after serving seven and a half year. With all of that being good time I was still denied my freedom. Flesh-Wound had prepared me for that probability. After being denied I thanked them for their time. I shook hands with the panelists who all said maybe next time. I had earned several certifications while and completed enough college courses to earn a degree. I learned from the man's books. I enhanced my mind and was taught by the very first man I ever knew.

I received a letter from my mother one day after being locked up for over eleven years. I don't know why I chose to open this one after so many years had come and gone, but it was pulling at me.

All is well my son, I pray that you are doing fine. After receiving your last letter over five years ago, I have tried to keep a promise that I made. I would never again write to you while you were locked up. Nic, it is hard as hell not to have seen you for all these years. Please explain to me why it is necessary for one to disengage this way.

I guess you've read that Lauren is expecting her third child and is married to…yes, he's a 'suit!' He is a wonderful man and they have lots of fun together.

Taylor is also married and has two children who are five and six. She's a housewife who teaches her children at home and has done very well by them.

I met a magnificent man two years ago and married him after only eight months. We are so happy together. Last but not least, Rae was also married shortly after you went to prison, but she lost her husband last year to cancer. They had a son who she proudly named guess what, son? Nic.

I couldn't finish the letter because I was growing weak from fighting back the tears conjured up by what I had just read. So much had happened without me being there. I was an uncle who had been absent from the lives of five nieces and nephews without me ever knowing it. Life on the outside was still evolving without me and it was time to refocus before I lost my emotional leverage. Flesh-Wound saw that the letter bothered me.

He said, "Youngster, why do you torture yourself this way? Didn't I teach you that for every action there would be a reaction? Stop beating yourself up over the head young man and understand that time heals all. Refocus and take your ass to sleep. Stop looking from side to side and concentrate on doing your time."

I thought about what he had said and allowed it to soak in. He taught me how to build a defense mechanism that would allow me to disengage from the general population. He taught me daily how to outthink and outsmart the so-called inquisitive thinkers of this world. For years now I had lived in a cell that was built for animals, but somehow by the grace of God, I had become a man. I had been eligible for parole three times over eleven years. I was locked up with the world's most dangerous human beings and forced to survive in the most hazardous conditions.

Although my incarceration was self-induced, I still believe that there has to be a better way to correct the wrongdoings of man. I came up for parole again and was granted my freedom at the age of thirty-one. The night before my parole hearing was bittersweet. I hadn't heard Flesh-Wound be more poetic than he was on that night.

"Youngster, thank you for never allowing my words to go unheard and for being strong enough to hold the torch of truth. Remember; never listen to negative gossip, for there are lies in the cruelty. Never be afraid to cry, for there is healing in a man's tears. Sometimes the moisture from them can be enough to put out the raging fires of frustration. Run if you must, from those who wish to extract your truths and replace them with their own."

In the thirteen years that I shared a cell with Flesh-Wound, he had never spoken my name once. I was always called Youngster. I could hear his voice weakening from the separation that was about to occur. "Nicoli, I've never had a child of my own, but if I did I would want a son like you. You are a light that this world must see, and I thank you for shining for me. When we met, you were just a boy who I watched become a man right before my eyes. I was offered good money to take my hands from around you, so that the animals inside these walls could molest your person. But the thought of such a thing would have persecuted my soul. No amount of money could have ever replaced the years we have spent together dining inside our souls as we both drank away the sorrows."

As Flesh-Wound spoke, I could see small tears forming in the corners of his eyes.

"Flesh, what if they tell me no?"

"They won't, Nicoli. You have paid your debt to society and your time here is over. I have one request though. After you get out, you must never try to contact me again. Do not even write me one letter," he instructed. I knew I would remember his orders.

I also knew that Flesh-Wound had the insight on the ins and outs of this prison, and if he told me I was going home, then I was.

I had called my mother two days earlier and asked her to attend her first parole hearing. She was overwhelmed by the call but promised that she would be there. I had become a trustee a couple of years prior, and I knew that would fair well with the parole board. I too felt that my time was drawing near and soon I would be a free man.

This time I would be able to walk the streets of the world and finally exist. The most mentally prepared man I knew had trained my mind. What I had seen in prison had revolutionized my stand in life. Going to jail had liberated me from my troubles and helped me sever ties to anger; anger which for years had imprisoned my soul. I knew that I would miss the long talks with Flesh-Wound, but it was time for me to go and teach someone else what I had learned.

I couldn't sleep and Flesh-Wound knew it, so we just stayed up talking and drinking Hennessey through the night. Flesh-Wound could get almost anything he wanted from the outside and he had often heard me talk about drinking Hennessey with my friends.

One of the many things that I had been taught while being locked up with the 'Truth' was not to replace an adjective where there could be a more meaningful word.

I was taught to use any recourse necessary to identify my core of reasoning. Everyday there was something to learn and Flesh-Wound saw to it that I did.

He had performed a mental operation upon my mind. He opened up the doors of my mind and withdrew the stupidity, which had aggravated my soul for years. He replaced it with a sense of brilliance. I was going to miss the only man I came to know and respect, but I planned to honor him on the outside as he had honored me over the years. He never really looked me directly in the eyes that night as he had taught me to do. I understood that he was dealing with my going home in his own way. So we drank and talked until I fell asleep. Early the next morning a guard banged on the cell door to wake me.

"Wake-up, Youngster. It's time to go to your parole hearing."

When I jumped down to tell Flesh-Wound good-bye, his bed was empty. He left a folded note with some pictures. I was feeling too sad to read it but knew I'd just read it later on my way home. When I picked up the note to place it inside my pocket, one of the pictures fell on the floor. It landed face down and the inscription on the back was a familiar one. It was my mother's handwriting. Suddenly it all came to me.

The man I had just spent the last thirteen with was Malik himself. After reading the back of the pictures I grew too weak to stand. What I was experiencing at that moment was unimaginable to the human mind. I had found my father and lived with him without ever knowing it. Those times listening to Flesh injecting his wisdom into my mind I had wished that he was my father not knowing that my wish had already come true. I had adopted his ways and knew that on the day I was to be set free, I would have to disconnect myself from my father, my friend.

A part of me wanted to commit a crime, so that I could live forever in endless harmony with my father. The first picture that I saw was of my mother holding me in her arms when I was a child. The next one was of me when I was about nine or ten years old. The last one was of me on my graduation day. Everything began to come together as I began to cry. I turned to the jailer and asked him to give me a couple of minutes. I needed time to absorb what I had just discovered. I sat back on Flesh's bunk and began to read the letter.

Good-bye Nicoli,

Do forgive me for not being there for the better part of your life. I lied to you when I told you that I never had a child of my own and today I know that I must finally put an end to this shameful lie. Nicoli, my real name is Malik Shabazz, and I am your father. I love you dearly. Never forget that. The circumstances by which we finally met were not the ones I hoped for, but over the years I pray that they've served their purpose.

Your mother told me that you were disturbed when you found out that I was alive, but that you never asked about me again. We never wanted it to be like this, but I guess life has a way of working things out for the better. Nicoli Walker, you are now fit to walk the streets of this world and teach the unlearned.

It was me who named you Nicoli, but ten days after you were born I was incarcerated. When she came to visit me I cried out to your mother through an inch and a half of glass. I begged her to tell you that I had died. I never wanted you to see me this way, so I stopped answering your mother's letters. It was not her fault, it was mine. If there is anyone to blame, it is me.

I was told that you were coming to this prison and I asked the warden to place you in my cell. The rest is history. Remember to stay focused and to never forget that you matter to me more than life itself. Tell Sam that I said hello and that I'm proud of the job she did with you. Be better to yourself than I was to me and remember old Flesh from time to time.

I love you, Youngster,
Flesh

    I wanted to leave a picture of me on his bed, but I knew that Flesh needed to stay focused. So I just took all of my things and walked with the guard towards what I hoped would be freedom. It took forever to get down to the center where the parole hearing was taking place but something was different about this walk. It felt like a great weight had been taken off my shoulders.

    There were a lot of brothers I had come to know over the years yelling out, 'Good-luck!' as I reached the bottom floor of a correctional facility. I looked back to wave.

    A guard turned and said, "He'll be back. Save that noise."

    I began smiling at him as I reflected on what my response towards his remark might have been years ago.

When we reached the parole center I was placed in a holding cell until it was my time to go in. I was more nervous about seeing my mother than I was about being released. I had become accustomed to letdowns and was immune to rejection. An older gentleman finally opened the door and told me to come in. My feet grew heavy and my heart stopped beating again like it did thirteen and a half years ago when I first arrived.

I got up out of my seat and walked into the room with my head held high like Flesh had told me to do. All I could see was the panel of three men and two women who would once again decide my fate. There was a wall to my right that I would have to clear before I saw my mother's face again.

I had two steps to go when I heard her. "Where is he?" she asked with a soft voice. Simultaneously I revealed myself and stood in front of the judgment panel.

I turned around, and to my surprise there stood my queens: my mother, Taylor, Lauren, even Rae. I was overwhelmed by their presence. I had done nothing to deserve their love up to this point in my life, but I vowed that if I were to be released, I would never let them down again.

I turned back to face the panel with jubilant heart and emotional freedom running through my veins.

"Mr. Walker, we have looked over your case and have found no reason why you shouldn't be released back into society. You have paid a tremendous price for the crime that you committed and this panel is satisfied with its findings.

"You seem remorseful and very apologetic about your actions on the night in question. Could you please stand and tell us what you would do if you were placed back into society?"

I stood up and looked them straight in the eyes.

"Good evening," I began. "When I first came here over thirteen years ago, my soul was hollow and my life had no substance. I hung out with the worst kind of people imaginable and before I knew it I became one of them myself. I turned my back on my queens and I let them down. I haven't seen them all these years, until today.

"My hair has started to gray and I have never even been employed. You ask me what would I do? I would attempt to fill the void that I've created in our lives. I would cry when my heart felt sad and teach my sister's children how to grow up and become strong vibrant young men and women."

I was told to go back into the waiting room but it wasn't five minutes before I was asked to return for the decision.

"Mr. Walker, this panel has never been as moved as it was today. Your selection of words has humbled us and we are delighted to tell you that you are now a free man. You are free to go and enjoy the rest of your life."

My 'Four Queens' were jumping up and down as I turned and waved at them. There was no touching while we were still in this section of the prison, so they were escorted back outside to wait for me. My release was announced over a loudspeaker and the inmates went crazy. I received a modest check and all of my belongings. It was odd to see the clothes that I was wearing back then.

"Hey, Nicoli. Here are some clothes that your mother brought for you."

It was just like my mother to have my clothes there waiting for me. She even had shoes to match my outfit and damn, was I sharp. I could tell the new styles would suit me just fine.

Before the final set of doors opened and closed behind me, I could feel Flesh-Wound staring at me from a room that was close to the front gate. His silhouette was waving good-bye. I waved back while the doors that would separate us forever were closing.

When the doors finally closed completely I walked towards my queens until my feet forced me to run. I embraced them all like never before. My new shirt was drenched with tears, but my heart was filled with tranquility. First I hugged my mother and then Lauren, Taylor and finally Rae. They were all still as beautiful as ever and Rae was just as poised as the last time I saw her. They came to pick me up in a van my mother had just bought with some of her retirement money. We had about 400 miles to catch me up on all of the news.

Lauren led off, "Nic, did you hear what happened to Do-Me?"

"No, I never watched TV or read the newspapers while I was locked up."

"What? What are you saying, son?" asked my mother.

"Some people do their time different from others. I chose to disconnect myself from the outside world, as I knew it. So tell me, what happened to Do-Me?"

"Lauren, Nic doesn't care to hear about that right now," my mother cautioned.

"No, it's okay. Go ahead and tell me," I insisted.

"Do-Me was killed in prison. He was found in his cell stabbed in the head forty-seven times with an ice pick.

"I heard that Stick was also killed in prison five years into his stretch. They said it was a Mafia-style execution," Lauren reported. I was told that some brothers beat him so bad that he lost the feeling in his face. They tied his hands behind his back, severed his penis, and then placed it in his mouth. His face was so numb that he couldn't push it out of his mouth. Someone found him wandering around naked, and bleeding to death."

They added that Chuck was 'the man' in prison. He had become the tank manager and was running things in his block. All the news left me empty.

"I'm sorry to hear that," was all I could say.

I thought that she was also going to add that my Uncle Leon died right after I was incarcerated, even though I already knew that. Flesh had taught me to turn down the madness and I began to do so as the van grew quiet.

Lauren broke the ice again and they began showing me pictures of their families. The mood changed from melancholy to upbeat in a matter of seconds. I became so emotional and started to cry.

"What's wrong?" asked Rae.

"Yes, what's wrong, Baby?" my mother asked.

"Everyone's so beautiful and I'm so happy for you all."

"Then why are you crying, Nic?" asked Taylor.

"I'm not crying tears of sadness, these are tears of joy and the feeling of reconnection. The type of tears that I couldn't have shed while in prison. I needed to see these pictures so that I could somehow touch your reality.

into a driveway. Everyone was getting out of the van, so I got out as well.

"Son, this is my home," my mother said. "Come on. Let's go in and meet everyone."

I knew nothing about this life, or about this world for that matter. But I was with my queens and I knew that they were with me.

"Go ahead and open the door, Nic," Taylor said.

When I reached to open the door, my hands grew cold and it took all the strength to turn the handle. When I did I heard a loud, "Surprise!!!"

As I stepped inside with my queens there were so many people waiting for us. Some I had never seen in my life. My mother called out for her grandchildren and they all came running to her.

They stood there staring at me and I paired up the children in my head. I could see each of their mother's in their eyes. None of them said a word before my mother told me their names.

I stopped her and said, "I'll learn their names, but let me try and guess whose children are whose. These two are Taylor's children. I can see that they are the teachers of our future. Now, those two are Lauren's. Am I guessing right? That has to be your third child Lauren that brother is holding."

Lauren turned to me and said, "You're smarter than I thought you were. My oldest son, Ronnie, is eight years old. That is Erica, and she is seven. And this is my youngest, Jermal." She continued by introducing her husband. "This is my husband, Eric. Eric, this is my brother, Nic."

"Pleased to met you, my brother," Eric said.

"This is Nic, my son and your new pupil. Teach him as you have been taught and never ask me how I know about the wisdom that you have acquired."

We must have hugged for five minutes, when suddenly someone else came through the door. I was shocked to recognize Tamara.

My mother took her hand and led her to me.

"Nicoli, I invited her here because I felt that she had something to tell you."

What in the world could she possibly have to tell me? After all I had only seen her once in my life.

My mother began the story. "I was in the supermarket one day when I over heard a woman calling out a familiar name. I walked over and introduced myself. I began to tell her that I too had a son by the same name..."

I interrupted, "But Mama, what are you saying?"

"Nic, you are a father and Tamara is the mother of your child. That night you two were together Tamara got pregnant. After having her baby; she told her child the same lie that I told you when you were born."

"No. What are you two saying?"

By that time Rae came out of a room down the hall holding the hand of someone that looked like me. My eyes could no longer fight back tears of joy.

Tamara looked at the youngster and said, "Please tell the man your name."

He looked up at me and said, "Nicoli is my name."

I ran over to him and began to stroke his face.

"Daddy, why are you crying? Aren't you glad to see me?"

I placed my hands on his shoulders and pushed him gently outwards just enough to look into his eyes. I said, "What I feel at this very moment, my son, is what I wished my father could have felt for me. Glad is not what I'm feeling. There has to be a better word for the magnitude of this moment. Although I have never seen you before, I love you more right now than anything in this world.

"Please never hate your mother for not telling you that I was alive. Try not to let anger creep into your heart. I will never leave you again, not as long as I am blessed to breathe. Sure, my son, I am glad to see you, but more than anything I am grateful."

All of my queens came over to me and we hugged as I held my son in my arms. I reached out for Tamara, motioning for her to join us.

She whispered in my ear, "I'm sorry, Nic."

I needed to know more about my son, so I asked Tamara to join me for a walk. Before we left the house I felt I owed my mother an apology. I walked over to her and said, "Mama, I know that you know who I have been locked up with all of these years."

She smiled at me and said, "Yes, how is he?"

"He is the greatest man I've ever known. I learned so much from him. He made me a man."

"I knew that you would. He was always a great conversationalist."

"Yes, that he is, but more than anything else, he is my father. Thanks for being who you are and for loving me the way you have all these years."

"Nic, I am the queen of all of your queens. I'm supposed to love you this way."

She smiled and kissed me on the cheek as we both laughed openly. She looked towards Tamara and said to me, "I think someone's waiting on you."

"That's right. I'll see you later, Mama. There are some questions that I need to ask her. We'll be right back."

While we were walking Tamara took my hand and placed it in hers.

"I never stopped thinking about you, Nic. I just didn't want my son's childhood to be destroyed."

I could overlook the fact she had never informed me of her situation. "What's going on in your life?" I asked her.

"Nothing really. I haven't been seeing anybody for over two years and I've never had anyone stay over at my house. I was married once for about eight months but he and Nicoli never got along, so we divorced."

"Something is different about you, Nic. Something in your eyes is pulling me towards you at this very moment. I know that it's too soon, but I wish that we could try and make it together as a family."

She was still as fine as ever and I hadn't been with a woman in years. In fact I had never been with another woman.

"Nicoli, I want you to come home with us tonight and stay there as long as you like. We have a home not too far from here that needs a man's attention."

"I would love to," I accepted and we kissed in agreement.

The three of us went home together that night as a family, and Tamara and I married soon after that.

might carry a word to heal our emotional wounds. Vengeance is not ours, for most of our wars are spiritual in nature. Many of us lack the biblical knowledge necessary to defeat the visual vessels that merely carry anger. The premise of an act is its root, and only there can it truly be destroyed.

He who says he has never been deceitful may be granted a special harvest of endless excruciating pain for telling such a lie. On the other hand, he who is willing to admit that he falls short of the glory of God will be blessed with the opportunity to right his wrongs. I never gave my mother this opportunity.

The Flesh-Wounds in this world are hard to come by, and many times the price of conversing with such a man shall cost more than you're willing to spend. Learn to forgive anyone who breathes the same air you breathe. Disrobe the spirit of stupidity and cleanse yourself as needed in the mental bath of peace and tranquility. Scrub hard if you must, but remove the dirty filth and rubbish of madness with determination. Hell is the destiny of a fool and heaven is the final resting place of a soul who fills his heart with the truth.

Afterword

While writing this, my first book, I knew preparing this passage would probably be the moment that would touch me the most. For years I have traveled through life without any words to call my own. The word "instrumental" has taken on a whole new meaning and has somehow created inside of me a foundation of hope. First of all I must thank You, Lord, for You are the true author of all that is real. Before I was born it was You who wrote my life and published it through my birth. I thank You for placing a vision inside my soul, powerful enough to reason with inadequacies.

I truly believed that my soul wasn't meant to be understood, for my words have never been my own and neither has my journey. I thank You for disabling my fears over the years and for replacing them with wisdom. I thank You for teaching me how to dissect lies and restore them with truth. Thank You for the many struggles You fed me intravenously from heaven; for without the nourishment of truth I would never have been able to taste a piece of triumph.

For My Mother

This book is dedicated to the driving
force in my life, my mother.
For never allowing me to remain on
the wrong side of the road.
Unlike my father, you remained strong
and carried your load.
Mama, I thank you for standing in front
of the storms and redirecting the winds.
I thank you for teaching me to
do whatever it morally takes,
Instilling inside my soul the
spirit to bend instead of break.
For all the things you allowed me to go through,
Those things you closed your eyes and simply
allowed me to grow through.
For those words you spoke in my lowest hour
And for being a mother with endless soothing power.
I thank you for feeding me out of the plates
of patience and the bowls of endurance.
For having enough insight to refill
my cup with "You've got to"
And for always saying "Son, you can win."
For giving me the chance to go it on my own
And knowing that by doing so it would
stiffen up my back and make me strong.
For setting me down at the table of truth,

forcing me to eat my morals
Teaching me that I must remain
focused through my sorrows.
For placing dignity inside
everything you dared to teach,
And for all of those times you
decided not to preach.
For setting the bar high
And teaching me that it's okay to defy.
This book is a small note that will
extend my love when it's needed
And please remember my shoulder
when you feel defeated.
When times got hard you could have run away,
This book was written to say,
"Thank you for deciding to stay!"

I love you, Mama.
I promised you one day, I'd learn to read.
Here's to keeping that promise.

YOUR SON,
Anthony 'DOC' Hamilton